What People A

PODCAST TO BROADCAST
Author Chris J. Witting Jr.

"Chris Witting's vast knowledge and experience in the industry is unparalleled. Over the past 8 years, he helped me build a network for my weekly radio show and was a driving force behind my popular podcast. This book is the next best thing to having Chris with you at every critical step in the process. His sterling reputation is based on integrity. In other words, everything you read in this book, you can take to the bank. By buying and reading this book you're taking your first steps to successful radio syndication."

Richard Syrett
Broadcaster/Podcaster
Guest Host - Coast to Coast AM

"If you've gone to the trouble of creating a great podcast, radio syndication provides an opportunity to reach many more listeners and develop a new revenue stream. In this book you'll discover the right path to take and the pitfalls to avoid. This is the manual for syndication success!"

Mike Carruthers
Host, Something You Should Know Podcast

"If you're a podcaster looking to grow your audience, have you ever thought about taking your show to RADIO? Radio reaches millions. In this book, Chris J. Witting offers the proven six step formula to help you successfully add *'syndicated radio host'* to your title."

Valerie Geller
Author, *Beyond Powerful Radio*
Broadcast/Podcast Coach

"Chris Witting pulls back the curtain and brilliantly reveals the secrets of how to expose your podcast to a much larger audience. If you have *ever* considered taking your podcast to the next level, all of your questions will be answered in this step-by-step guide to broadcast success."

Chris Berry
Executive VP News/Talk and Sports, iHeart Media

"While the vast majority of podcasters struggle to generate sufficient revenue, radio syndication has a very profitable business model. PODCAST TO BROADCAST is an essential guidebook for podcasters who want to test the waters of syndication."

Hiram Lazar
CFO, Compass Media Networks

"Chris Witting and the people at Syndication Networks helped me launch my podcast in 2017. They were instrumental in the start of my nationally syndicated radio show in 2019. I highly recommend them to anyone who wants to take their podcast to syndication. Chris and his team can make it happen."

Leonard Birdsong
Host of The Urban Connection

"PODCAST TO BROADCAST will show you how to take your podcast to the next level, and capture the larger audiences and income that radio syndication can provide. Chris Witting's reputation and experience in the radio industry speaks for itself, he has a proven track record of mentoring hosts to success in radio syndication."

Charles Steinhauer
Chief Operating Officer of Westwood One

"I've been working with Chris Witting and Syndication Networks for years, in fact they've been syndicating my show from the very beginning. Chris and his staff work very hard to make sure the results are there, signing up stations to carry my show. They have been very, very good at doing that for me."

Carl Amari
Host of Hollywood 360 Radio

About Chris J. Witting, Jr.

 **Chris J. Witting, Jr.** is CEO of Syndication Networks Corporation (SNC), the Chicago-based syndication consulting and marketing company. He is the only syndication consultant in America who is a current, successful host of multiple syndicated radio shows, and who also has experience as a major market general manager and program director. His career in radio includes top stations in New York, Chicago, Philadelphia, Boston, and other markets.

His daily syndicated program, *The Success Journal*, is heard in over 100 markets. The award winning show spawned a popular book (*21-Day Countdown to Success* published by Career Press), a weekly national TV segment, speaking engagements, and over 100 interviews on radio and television. Chris also hosts *InfoTrak*, a weekly interview show heard on over 700 stations as well as the daily syndicated medical feature, *Check Up On Health*.

Syndication Networks has a talented staff with a combined 150 years of experience in syndication. Its clients include podcasters, radio hosts, producers and networks seeking larger audiences and greater income.

Syndication Networks Corp. has been in business since 1993, with an established online presence since 1996. Consistently top Google-Ranked for radio syndication, SNC offers its nearly 2,000 affiliate stations a wide array of quality syndicated content. SNC is the leading online resource for hosts and producers seeking syndication consulting and information.

Note from the Author

We first formulated the "Six Steps to Successful Syndication" over 20 years ago and happily, these rules have stood the test of time. Our Syndication.net web site first listed the immutable Six Steps way back in the year 2000 (see the Internet Archive). It's highly gratifying that many others have picked up on the Six Steps to Syndication over the years.

We've been advising people who want to syndicate since 1995 ...which is like 30 billion "media years." In other words, we've been helping people deal with these exact same issues for over 25 YEARS. Last we checked, most of the "syndication experts" have bought some of our trainings. But as a reader of *Podcast To Broadcast*, you've come straight to the source. If you're ready to syndicate yourself, there's no question this book can help you. Read on.

PODCAST TO BROADCAST

The Six Step Formula to Turn Your Podcast into a Profitable, Nationally Syndicated Radio Show

By Chris J. Witting Jr.

Author of *Syndication Nation*

FREE - STRATEGY CALL

This Book Includes a Free Strategy Call You Can Use RIGHT NOW to Get Started in Syndication.

Get It NOW at

http://SyndicationInfo.com

Podcast To Broadcast: The Six Step Formula to Turn Your Podcast Into a Profitable, Nationally Syndicated Radio Show

ISBN 978-0-9640347-5-4

Published by Harmony House
616 N North Court, Ste 200
Palatine, IL 60067

Table of Contents

The Product Ladder

Positioning Your Show

What to Never Say

Life of a Program Director

What to Do If You're New

Chapter 11 – Ingredients of a Killer Demo   97

High Production Value

Start with a Montage

A Great Sample Show

Add a Strong Close

Include Your Contact Info

Chapter 12 – Income from Your Show 103

Barter Advertising

Minimum National Audience

Value Depends on Audience Size

National Sales Representation

Chapter 13 – System for Ad Sales 109

The Multi-step Process

Nothing Comes From Nothing

Common Misperceptions

Friends and Family

Prepare Before You Pitch

Dig Deep In Your Niche

Research Possible Advertisers

Research Your Audience

Online Listener Survey

Chapter One

Why Radio Syndication?

Since you're reading these words, you're probably a podcaster – or at least, you have a serious interest in podcasting. Smart move! Podcasting is one of the fastest-growing forms of media ever created. Audiences and advertising revenues appear to be soaring to the sky, and the growth opportunities seem endless. Plus, the barriers to entry are incredibly low for new podcasts and the next generation of podcasting superstars.

So why on God's green earth would anyone ever be interested in adding old-fashioned broadcast radio to their podcast distribution platform? After all, radio is one of the oldest forms of electronic media. It's been around for 100 years. Does anyone still listen to the radio?

The answer to that last question is YES. Radio has hundreds of millions of listeners every week in the United States.

Recent national audience research from Nielsen says that broadcast radio reaches over 90% of the U.S. population every week – that's well over 200 million listeners. That is greater reach than television.

Thanks to radio's massive (and responsive) audience, radio advertisers spend close to **twenty billion dollars a year** to get their messages heard on those old-fashioned airwaves (data as of 2019).

Meanwhile, annual revenues from podcasting are a small fraction of what radio pulls in. Total podcast ad spending is **less than $500 million a year** (as of 2019).

In short, radio offers the two things that every podcast host dreams of: more listeners and more ad dollars.

"I feel like everybody's podcasting and nobody's podlistening."

So the question really is, why wouldn't every smart podcaster look for ways to expand their reach and their revenue, by exploring national radio syndication? It only makes sense.

Audience Size

Picture yourself standing on the stage of a giant amphitheater or arena filled to the brim with people. It's standing room only and all those people are there to hear you speak. How many people would that be in total? Thirty five thousand, fifty thousand, or maybe seventy thousand in a giant arena? That's a lot of people. But the fact is, it's not so big compared to the audience of national radio. Your radio audience could be 10 to 20 times larger, or more. Imagine what it would feel like to speak to an audience of that enormity, and imagine the potential response of that massive listening audience.

A Real Life Example

If you have a national radio audience numbering five million and you really connect with just **one percent** of them through your words and ideas, how many people would that be? Well, let's do the math: that's 50,000 people. Would 50,000 active and involved listeners positively impact your success? You'd better believe they would. Successful syndicated broadcasters get these levels of audience response.

Consider one actual example. A syndicated radio talk show host decided to start a listener newsletter. He began to promote it during the show.

In a short time, his newsletter subscription orders exploded in volume. That newsletter quickly became one of the fastest-growing non-financial newsletters in America, and it earned the syndicated host a great deal of money.

Sharing a Story

As we begin, here is the brief story of our own syndication success. It all began with a show titled The Success Journal®, airing on one radio station. It's now heard in over 100 markets nationwide, and on American Forces Radio worldwide. (We also host two other syndicated shows, InfoTrak® and Check Up On Health.)

And as we said, that first show began on one station, on the weekends. You may be wondering how it grew from a weekly show on one station to become a daily show heard in 100 markets. We're going to share that information with you, but let's not get ahead of ourselves.

People ask if doing a syndicated radio show has been a positive experience. The answer is "Absolutely, yes!" There are many great benefits that can come from syndication.

A successful syndicated radio show can generate a substantial income for the host. For example, The Success Journal® has earned well over one million dollars in advertising income. Now please understand, we're not claiming you will earn that much, or any amount, from syndication. But the fact remains, a popular syndicated show can earn a very good income. We'll explore the financial benefits of syndication in the pages ahead.

We experienced another benefit from syndication, and it began about six months after the show went national.

We launched a catalog of products related to the show. This decision was driven by listener requests. People wanted copies of the broadcasts, along with other motivational audio products. We made these items easy to order, and we offered a wide variety of products. We set up a toll-free line and catalog orders came from all over the US.

When we set out to design the catalog, we took the advice of a friend who sold products using a catalog. He provided coaching and advice, and his tips helped us avoid many common pitfalls.

There's an old saying, "If you want to succeed at something, follow the advice of a person who successfully did that same thing." Well, that's just what we did, and that rule worked well. Now you may not have considered selling products or opening an online store, but it's something you may want to think about if you pursue radio syndication.

But let's not put the cart before the horse. We'll touch on the concept of selling products related to your show in a later chapter.

Benefits of Syndication

A nationally syndicated show can be a platform for many ventures. Here are some other ways we benefited from our coast-to-coast radio show.

After launching the catalog, communication with listeners continued. That led to the next project: a book about success. The book profiled successful people heard on the radio show, and it explored their success strategies. As a first-time author, advice from an expert was essential. We reached out to someone who authored a popular non-fiction book, and he agreed to be our mentor. Thanks to him, we learned that there are best practices to follow when it comes to writing non-fiction, and you need to apply those rules.

We sent our book proposal to a literary agent, and shortly thereafter signed a deal with a well-known publishing company. We got that deal in a matter of weeks. Typically, an unproven first-time author can struggle, sometimes for many months, to get a book deal with a reputable publisher. Our deal came through very quickly, primarily because we host a syndicated radio show. And we know this to be a fact, because the publisher later told us so.

The book drew endorsements from many people, including Mark Victor Hansen (co-author of *Chicken Soup for the Soul)*, millionaire CEO Lillian Vernon, brain training expert Jose Silva, *Parade Magazine* editor Walter Anderson, and many others. These were all people we connected with through our syndicated radio show.

You can find that book, *21-Day Countdown to Success,* on Amazon.com. It has been republished worldwide, in multiple languages.

So far, we've described the financial rewards, the product sales, the book, and the testimonials.

But there were more benefits that came to us from radio syndication.

- We were invited to host a weekly national cable TV feature on the TLN cable network.

- We appeared on Fox TV, NBC TV, CNN Financial News, and many more.

- We were asked to write articles for national publications such as *Success Magazine*, which, of course, were paid gigs.

- A widely read trade magazine invited us to write a weekly business column.

If all this wasn't enough, there are just a few more things we'll quickly mention.

- We were booked to deliver keynote speeches before large audiences.

- We hosted corporate seminars for Fortune 100 companies.

All this is not to brag or boast. We are sharing these facts just to point out the many ways that national radio syndication can provide you with new opportunities.

Podcast Facts of Life

Now maybe you're thinking, "Yes, but all these same things can happen just by doing a podcast!"

Well, yes, that's true. But getting noticed as a podcast host is far more challenging than it is for a syndicated radio host. Here's why.

As of 2020, Apple Podcasts is reportedly home to over **one million podcasts.** It's estimated that about half of these are in active production. This means that your podcast has about 500,000 active competitors in the podcast universe at any given time. So a podcast faces challenging odds of becoming even a minor national hit against so many competitors.

So Many Podcasts

World-famous podcaster Joe Rogan made headlines when he cashed in his podcast rights for $100 million. Keep in mind, his podcast was ranked number one, ahead of 999,999 podcast competitors. No matter how entertaining or compelling your podcast may be, chances are it won't be taking over Joe's #1 position anytime soon. Nothing personal, it's just a matter of numbers.

There is a vast universe of podcasts chasing listeners and ad dollars. According to My Podcast Reviews, at least 50,000 brand new podcasts are launched every single month. This just adds to the massive competition you face in this relatively new medium.

No Barrier to Entry

Why are there so many podcasts? One obvious reason: the barrier to entry for new podcasts is almost non-existent. It's extremely easy to record your voice. Most laptops have built-in microphones. Or, you can simply use your smart phone to record yourself. Next, choose one of the many podcast distribution platforms, such as LibSyn or Blubrry. Upload your show, and presto! You are now a podcaster.

As we said, there's virtually no barrier to entry.

The 11 year-old kid next door can launch a podcast in his bedroom just as easily as a top industry professional can produce her podcast at a fancy recording studio. People of all ages, and from all walks of life, are starting podcasts every single day.

The Syndication Comparison

There is a huge difference in the numbers between radio syndication and podcasting.

Simply put, there are far fewer nationally syndicated radio talk shows than there are spoken word podcasts.

While we are not aware of official statistics, according to the industry professionals we spoke with, here is an educated guess. There are **fewer than 1,500** syndicated radio talk shows available to broadcast radio stations at any given time.

Compare that figure to the number of podcasts in active production. You can plainly see the massive competitive difference between national radio and podcasting.

This should encourage you, if you are thinking about taking your podcast to syndicated radio.

Loads of Content

The number of FCC licensed, full time radio stations across America varies slightly each month. Stations sign on or sign off for various reasons.

Here's a conservative estimate: 10,000 US radio stations are on the air full time. We're talking about commercial radio stations, licensed to broadcast 24 hours a day, seven days a week, 52 weeks a year.

How many hours of program content does it take to keep all these stations on the air?

24 hours x 7 days x 52 weeks x 10,000 stations = 87,366,000 hours!

It's an astonishing number, but the number is very real. Full time American radio stations need almost **90 million hours of content** every year to fill their airwaves. Yet the trend at most stations is toward reduced budgets and limited staffing.

With so many hours to fill, and rapidly shrinking rosters of on-air talent, how do all these stations fill the massive programming gap?

If you guessed syndication, you're right. A primary source of quality content for many thousands of broadcast stations is radio syndication. Stations are always on the lookout for new, innovative, entertaining shows, more today than ever before.

The Demand Factor

There is another difference between podcasting and radio syndication, what we'll call "The Demand Factor".

Consider these questions. How much demand can there realistically be for one more podcast, when 50,000 new podcasts are being created every single month? Is anyone really asking for podcast number 50,001? Do you know anyone who has the time to listen to 100 podcasts, much less 50,000 of them?

Being charitable, one might say the novelty factor for new podcasts is not what it once was. That's not to say a new podcast hosted by someone famous doesn't attract attention. Likewise, a major media company's newest podcast may create some buzz. But the vast majority of podcasts are not hosted by big names nor do they come from top networks. Most of these typical podcasts get overlooked by most of the listeners and advertisers.

Meanwhile, changes are happening among the big players in the podcasting industry. Podcast networks have begun to consolidate. New formats are being tested. Some hosts are switching to subscription models. These changes may leave independent podcasters even further out of the mainstream, where there is even less demand for new podcasts.

Certainly, some podcasts have become huge hits buoyed by strong listener interest. But there's only so much room at the top. A significant number of today's top podcasts launched early in the game, when there was less competition. Others enjoy the backing of large media organizations, to their great advantage. This makes it more difficult than ever for independent podcasters to break through into the top ranks.

What's Your Demand Factor?

How much listener demand exists for your podcast -- especially if you aren't already a household name, or don't have an inside connection, or haven't signed an exclusive deal with one of the big boys?

If you're among the vast majority of podcasters, demand for your podcast is probably minimal. Yes, you may have collected dozens of good reviews on iTunes. You may have thousands (or even tens of thousands) of downloads per episode. But so have countless others. Unfortunately, those numbers don't mean what they used to.

The bottom line: The Demand Factor for most podcasts just isn't significant. And with a constant barrage of new podcasts saturating the market, it isn't easy for an individual podcaster to find listeners and ad revenues. This leaves many independent producers on their own, trying to grow against challenging odds.

Syndication Demand

We believe there is a much higher Demand Factor for quality shows in radio syndication.

Author Ben Shapiro hosted a daily political podcast. There are thousands of other political podcasts in production, and his was just one against many. But in 2018, Shapiro's podcast jumped to radio syndication. By 2019 his show was heard in 200 markets, including nine of the top ten markets. His switch to radio resulted in a massive boost in listeners, influence, and income.

While this is an exceptional case, it does illustrate that with good content, a quality podcast can make the successful leap to radio syndication. In radio, the demand remains strong for fresh, quality programming.

Let's repeat that thought. If your goal is to reach a larger number of listeners and potentially earn a substantial income from your show, there is demand for fresh, new shows in radio syndication. As long as you can consistently create quality content, your show can be completely independent and need not be affiliated with a major network or a wealthy underwriter to succeed in radio.

One example of this is The Dave Ramsey Show. Ramsey's primary focus is personal financial freedom. The show has been independently produced from the very beginning. Ramsey's show began on one station, and he chose to self-syndicate. He learned syndication from the ground up. Today, The Dave Ramsey Show is heard five days a week on over 500 stations. The show generates millions of dollars in annual income and has spawned a financial services empire.

Independents Can Win

Solo show hosts can be very successful in radio syndication. We observe this at our syndication company, where each week, stations across America sign up to carry the shows we represent. The majority of our shows are not hosted by anyone famous, nor do they have big marketing budgets.

Nor do we pay a dime to any radio station for the airtime. All our shows are placed on stations on a barter commercial basis (see Chapter 12 for an explanation of barter).

What attracts radio station's interest in our shows? We offer unique, quality content that has good production values, with show hosts that are passionate about entertaining and informing their listeners.

If you are capable of producing a good show on a consistent basis, you owe it to yourself to seriously explore radio syndication. There's no guarantee you will become a syndication superstar like Dave Ramsey or Ben Shapiro, but The Demand Factor is definitely healthy in national radio.

Musical Freedom

We'll close this chapter with one more advantage that radio syndication has over podcasting. If you want to legally include music in a podcast, you either have to pay a rights fee for each song, hire someone to compose and perform the music for your show, or resign yourself to using royalty-free music tracks. But on radio, you have musical freedom. You can use any licensed popular music without paying a dime. This is because radio stations enjoy grandfathered licensing deals with ASCAP and BMI. So if you want to rock out with the latest hits or appeal to adult listeners with golden oldies, you have the freedom to do so with a syndicated radio show.

Chapter Two

Beginnings of Syndication

If you're someone who enjoys having historical perspective, this chapter is for you. But if you don't care to know how today's types of radio syndication evolved, and just want to jump directly to the how-to chapters, you can skip ahead. But to fully understand the state of syndication today, and to have some perspective on what's involved, we believe it is very helpful to know its evolution.

While radio syndication might seem to be a modern day concept that began in the era of countdown music shows and high profile talk shows, it actually has its roots in the early decades of the last century.   Let's briefly go back to that time, to see how it began.

After radio's first commercial broadcast on November 2, 1920 when KDKA Pittsburgh aired live coverage of that year's presidential election returns, radio station licenses were soon being handed out like crazy to entrepreneurs across America.   This was a bit like the wild and crazy early days of the Internet with service providers and new websites springing up everywhere.

At many of these early, independent stations, revolutionary thinkers had new ideas. They pioneered previously undreamed of ways to use radio, such as the first live broadcast of a church service, the first play-by-play of live football, live baseball, live auto racing, live horseracing, and so on.   On-location news broadcasts at first amazed listeners, but the live shots became commonplace as clever technicians figured out how to tackle seemingly insurmountable technological challenges.

As an example, back in the early days, radio used primitive control board technology. This meant that something like a live broadcast of a church service was only possible by placing ugly, bulky equipment right in front of the altar. For obvious reasons, this seemed impossible until an engineer realized he could wear a choir robe and sing along with the choir, while running the equipment which was hidden behind a panel. This sort of inventive thinking happened at every level in the fast-growing radio industry.

The Impossible Seemed Possible

As we mentioned, radio's earliest days somewhat paralleled the wild and wooly early years of the Internet, when impossible ideas seemed possible to cutting-edge minds. New breakthroughs happened daily. As radio grew in the public consciousness during that era, audiences exploded and visionaries capitalized on those new listeners.

It soon became clear that once the novelty of hearing voices and music through the ether became common, radio's biggest ongoing expense was the endless creation of fresh, high-quality radio programming.

While a station's programs on a particular day might be of the very highest entertainment value, as soon as those programs were transmitted to listeners, all of that time, effort, and manpower was instantaneously rendered valueless.

This meant the station's staff had to start completely fresh the next day -- and the next, day after day, after day.

Feeding a Hungry Monster

No matter how good that day's programs might have been, it was all for naught once the broadcast day came to a close. Another full slate of programming had to be created from scratch. It was like feeding an insatiable monster whose appetite was never satisfied.

Thanks to Edison and other inventors, the phonograph and other recording devices already existed. So it was relatively easy for a radio station to record and save the audio of its high quality broadcasts. But no station worthy of respect from the audience would constantly rebroadcast the programs it had already presented, no matter how great those shows were.

Hundreds of new stations were coming on the air every year, and the radio industry was rapidly becoming a competitive battlefield. Popular talent was quickly put under contract. Top bandleaders were signed to exclusive deals. Stations moved fast to lock in the stars the public liked, in order to become masters of their programming destiny in the turbulent radio wars across the country.

Listeners expected to hear a fresh lineup of entertainment or drama every single day on their local stations. They would reject any station that re-ran old shows (unlike today when quite a few media channels simply recycle old shows). Back in those days, every effort was made to keep audiences glued to their radios with fresh content. No wonder they called it the golden age of radio!

Early Radio Syndication

It wasn't long until radio networks sprang up to distribute quality shows to the stations that couldn't afford to create fresh shows. In fact, some of today's big alphabet networks, CBS and NBC, became players back in the early decades of radio.

Not every small-town station was linked by wire to a network. In those pre-satellite days, new shows arrived at stations on transcription disks. The producers of these shows had to record and duplicate them on phonograph records, and ship the discs to stations. This was the earliest form of radio syndication, and it was incredibly successful. It worked so well, that radio stations were still receiving and airing syndicated shows on phonograph records right up to the early 1980s. In other words, this form of syndicated distribution continued for over 50 years!

Alongside the old mainstay of phonograph records, other means of distribution and syndication sprang up. For many years, stations received live shows and sports over AT&T long-distance lines. Commercial satellites remain an important form of syndicated distribution to this day. Note that satellite distribution of syndication is not to be confused with the consumer service, Sirius/XM satellite radio. The syndication sent to radio stations uses a completely different satellite system, not accessible to the public.

And let's not forget old school cassettes and reel-to-reel tapes, which for many years were used for program delivery to stations. Our show *The Success Journal*® was originally distributed to stations on tape. Today it is delivered to stations by digital download.

Classic Radio Shows

Perhaps you've heard old-time radio shows like *Dragnet*, *The Shadow*, *Fibber McGee and Molly,* and others. One of the most successful examples of early radio syndication involved a show produced at a Detroit radio station. It's one you've probably heard of: *The Lone Ranger*. The show was produced each week and broadcast locally. It was very popular, so producers wondered if it might do well with a national audience.

The producers of *The Lone Ranger* were not part of a radio network. So they chose to be independent and distribute the show to stations coast to coast. Thanks to the production value of the show (which included the William Tell overture as the musical theme), *The Lone Ranger* became a monster hit in syndication. It is still remembered today, many decades later. *The Lone Ranger's* impact on American culture will probably never be forgotten.

Think about that. While perhaps hundreds of other well-produced, cleverly written, highly original local radio shows from the same era are completely lost to history, never to be heard again, some like *The Lone Ranger* are etched in our collective memory because they chose national syndication.

Independent Self-Syndication

You may think it is risky to enter today's radio syndication marketplace. But imagine the risks for independents, back when the process was relatively unproven. Audio distribution was downright primitive. It meant shipping fragile 78 RPM disks to stations every week. Those disks had to be laboriously duplicated with typed or handwritten labels. Selling ads in those shows could be challenging as well. Until a show could prove it had listeners, it was much safer for advertisers to put their money elsewhere.

Certain themes or topics could be misunderstood or even offensive in parts of the country back then, but acceptable elsewhere. Writers had to use special care to create scripts that would be OK for a national audience.

Keep in mind we're talking about the radio world of the 1930s and 1940s, not radio today. Back in those days, the challenges of syndication didn't stop the producers of *The Lone Ranger* from entering the game. They became wealthy thanks to their risk-taking, while earning a place in the hearts and minds of millions with their program.

Modern Day Syndication

Much has changed in radio syndication since the early days of the business, but the basics remain the same.

Today, many thousands of radio stations are open to all kinds of syndication. These stations eagerly embrace new shows on a daily or weekly basis, which fuels the growth of this multi-billion-dollar industry.

Thanks to advances in technology, show distribution to stations has become routine. These include FTP downloads and XDS satellite distribution. Syndication ad sales are efficient and financially rewarding. Major advertisers put their dollars in syndication. And leading syndicators (such as our own Syndication Networks) provide independent hosts with full service syndication. All a host needs to do is create their show.

What hasn't changed is the need for quality content that appeals to a national audience.

Only for a Privileged Few?

Today's modern syndication is a far cry from the wild and wooly days of old-time radio. Yet to many podcasters, radio syndication is like some kind of secret fortress, accessible only to those who hold the keys to the kingdom. It appears to serve only a privileged few, the media kingpins and lucky insiders.

The sad reality is that many great podcasts are only reaching miniscule audiences. The hosts invest precious time and energy creating their podcasts. But they get no meaningful payback. If these podcasts were available for national radio syndication, they might entertain and inform many more listeners, while at the same time reaping rewards for the hosts.

Taking this point even further, there are many potential ideas for new shows -- concepts waiting to be produced, developed, marketed, and brought forth into reality -- by their imaginative creators. But these show concepts are going nowhere, simply because the dreamers haven't taken the steps to follow through.

Now you may think that this last point is just speculation on our part. But we assure you, at our company, we hear from people all the time telling us about clever, creative, unusual, and often exciting concepts for new syndicated programs. Sadly, most of these enthusiastic people who talk about their ideas never follow through. They don't even take the very first steps necessary to see if their ideas are viable.

What about you? If you think your podcast or show may have potential for syndication, please read on.

Chapter Three

Three Ways to Syndicate

There are three basic options to choose from, if your goal is to syndicate your podcast.

Solo Self-Syndication

The first way to do it is to do everything yourself by self-syndicating your show. That's how we first entered the business, when we initially began. And if we can do it, obviously you can too. But frankly, it can be a challenge if you aren't sure of what you're doing.

So if you go the self-syndication route, we first recommend learning all you can to avoid mistakes. You'll want to read this book from cover to cover, and then seek out additional knowledge resources (such as *Syndication Nation*, a 250 page book we wrote on the subject).

Hire an Employee

The second way to syndicate is to hire a person to do most of the work for you. This could be a skilled employee with media experience, or even a talented family member. That person's primary job is to sit at a desk (or the kitchen table) and contact radio stations every day, pitching the show to Program Directors, and signing up new stations to carry your show.

The employee can of course assist you with other matters, such as ad sales, distribution of your show, and so on. Alternatively, you could farm out each of the tasks to freelancers. For example, one person could contact stations to pitch them the show. Another person will sell ads. A third will manage show distribution to stations. Yet another will create marketing material, write press releases and so on.

Find a Partner

The third way to syndicate is to partner with a syndicator or network that offers full service, turn-key syndication. Full service usually means the company will handle almost everything, from creating a custom show demo, to marketing your show to stations, signing up stations, selling the ads, inserting the ads into your show, doing the billing and paperwork, sending invoices to advertisers, sending you payments, giving you progress reports, and more. All you do is host the show and they do the rest. These companies typically charge a fee or a commission on ad sales to pay for their services.

Podcasting Is Not Broadcasting

No matter how you choose to handle the syndication project, you need to understand the nuts and bolts of making your podcast accessible and attractive to broadcast radio stations.

Keep in mind, while podcasting and radio broadcasting are both forms of audio content, they are different types of media. The typical podcast, right out of the box, will not be compatible with broadcast syndication. So the next chapter will explore the steps to make your podcast fit the broadcast radio model. We call this the **Six Steps to Successful Syndication**.

Chapter Four

Content Creation

Here are the **Six Steps to Successful Syndication** we will explore in the pages ahead:

- Chapter Four - Content Creation
- Chapter Five - Format for Syndication
- Chapter Six - Get On the Air, Anywhere
- Chapter Seven - Demo and Branding
- Chapter Eight - Sign Up Stations
- Chapter Nine - Take Care of Business

Radio syndication is not rocket science, but there are specific steps to follow to syndicate your podcast. The first step to successful syndication is obvious. You must create content that will be appropriate for radio broadcasting. Sounds easy enough, right?

The key phrase in the sentence above is "appropriate for radio broadcasting". Most radio stations reach broad audiences. A successful syndicated show will be enjoyed by a good cross-section of the population. If you are convinced that the topic of your podcast already appeals to a fairly wide audience, congratulations! That's a good start.

But if your podcast is devoted to a micro-topic (and there are some podcasts like this), you will need to expand and broaden out the subject matter if you want a chance of making it in syndication.

Notice we did not say you need to "dumb it down". The show can be as intellectual and sophisticated as you wish, but the topic of discussion must attract the interest of a fairly wide audience of listeners.

Wide vs. Narrow Appeal

Here are some examples of wide and narrow topics. If you do a podcast about sports, you can legitimately focus on any popular sport such as football, basketball, hockey, and so on. Any of these would be an ideal overall show theme. Your individual episodes can delve into specific teams, players, coaches, etc. But if your show's entire overall focus and the total podcast series only examines one specific team or one single player, that will probably be too narrow for national radio.

Here's another example. Let's say your podcast is about the challenges of raising kids and being a parent. That's a great overall topic that has wide appeal to listeners and sponsors. It offers many different show ideas. But if your podcast tells the ongoing story of just one family or one individual child, this will likely prove too limited for broadcast radio.

One more example: a podcast about true-life crimes could be popular with many radio listeners. But a series of podcasts that only recounts the story of one crime or one criminal may be too narrow for wide radio acceptance.

Generally speaking, radio stations prefer non-fiction shows in choosing spoken-word syndication (although there are exceptions to this rule).

Watch Your Mouth

Let's mention another salient point here. Podcast content can resemble the Wild West in terms of language and topics. Podcasting is not licensed or regulated. There are virtually no legal limits on what can be said on a podcast (although libel and slander can still get you in serious trouble).

Broadcast radio stations operate under FCC licenses. As such, profanity and X-rated content are not allowed over the air. For this reason, it's best if your podcast is mostly "family friendly" in content. You should also understand libel and slander to avoid legal landmines.

What Appeals to You?

As you consider the specific topics your podcast will cover, think about what aligns with your personal interests and talents. Your best chance of success will happen if you choose a topic or theme that is interesting to you. Ideally, it should inspire you and ignite your passion. Whether you have prior broadcasting experience or not doesn't much matter. What does matter is having real interest in the subject matter of your show. Don't choose a topic for your show just because it looks like a way to make a fast buck in syndication. It is nice to earn money, but you will improve your odds of success by choosing a topic that you love to talk about.

On Demand vs. On The Fly

Podcast episodes offer on-demand flexibility for new listeners. A podcast listener can start with episode one, and then listen to each subsequent episode from start to finish, beginning to end. This works especially well if your podcast episodes tell a multi-part story.

But in most cases, radio listeners don't have this listening flexibility. They usually cannot go back to hear previous radio episodes they missed. Nor can they capture and store an entire series of radio shows for on demand listening. Instead, each radio episode must stand on its own. Your radio audience has to tune in to hear you on their local station at the right time. In other words, they hear you "on the fly" versus "on demand".

For this reason, the story arc concept of some very popular podcasts may not translate well to broadcast radio. However, podcasts that are produced with modular, stand-alone episodes are ideal for radio. If this episodic approach matches the style of your podcasts, you're in excellent shape for syndication. If not, you may want to consider reformatting the structure of your podcast so each episode can stand alone, without the need to refer back to past episodes to make sense of things.

Compatible Content Creation

We are still on Step One of the Six Steps to Syndication, and we're covering a lot of ground because compatibility with radio is one of the most important keys to success.

Let's turn to a proven formula to fine-tune a show concept for maximum acceptance by the radio audience. You should have a unique, memorable niche for your show that's different enough from the other syndicated shows that are out there.

Notice we said, "different enough." Here's an example of what we mean.

Let's say you do a podcast on health, and you plan to do your syndicated radio show on the same topic. Well, there are already a number of health talk radio shows on the air. So you must decide what will make your show unique and different from those others.

The 10 Percent Rule

You don't need to be totally unique. Here's a good rule of thumb. Just look at what's working out there already. Find a working concept, and improve on it by just 10 percent. See what we're saying? If your show is just 10 percent better than the competition, it will probably be a winner.

Here's an example from TV history to explain what we mean. There was a popular TV show in the 1960s called *Wagon Train*. It was a western about people traveling across the prairie on a wagon train, and all the adventures that happened along the way. Some years later, a TV producer named Gene Roddenberry noticed the success of *Wagon Train*. He took the concept of *Wagon Train* and changed the setting from the old west to outer space, and named the new show *Star Trek*. Again, it had the same basic concept and plot, with one significant location change. Roddenberry publicly admitted that *Star Trek* took the main concept of *Wagon Train*, but it was in a very different setting.

This strategy works. Countless TV shows, radio shows and books have followed this path to success. You might apply the same technique in conceptualizing your ideal syndicated radio show. Look at what's working out there already, and improve upon it by 10 percent. You will really improve your chances of winning.

How can you explore the competitive radio shows in your particular niche? In most cases, you can find the episodes online. Many will be posted on You Tube or on the host's website.

Gift of Gab

Now let's briefly touch on your qualifications as a syndicated host. There are successful hosts of syndicated radio shows who have never hosted a podcast or radio show in the past. Basically, if you enjoy talking with others, if people say you have the gift of gab, and if you feel a degree of passion for your subject matter (as we have mentioned), that's what it takes to make it. It also helps to have a sense of humor, both on and off the air.

A friend of ours describes herself as being a "talky" person, even in early childhood. Sure enough, she has had a very successful career in talk radio. Adding to her success is her ability to closely listen to others. Your show will benefit when you learn to listen to everything your co-hosts, guests and callers have to say. Two-way communication is the essence of good talk radio.

Chapter Five

Format for Syndication

When it comes to the length and format of a podcast, there really are no set rules. A podcast may be any length. And its length may vary considerably from episode to episode. The frequency in which new podcast episodes are released can vary as well.

The very opposite is true in radio syndication. Stations expect each episode to conform to a standard length with precise timing. So if you're used to ending your podcast whenever you run out of things to say, or wrapping things up around 35 minutes or so, neither of those will work for radio. You will need to watch the clock and make sure your podcast ends "on the button" each time. This isn't difficult once you get used to doing it.

You also need to produce new episodes at least once per week on a regular, predictable schedule. Doing a new episode "when you feel like it", or once or twice a month, won't work for radio. Standard schedules for syndicated radio shows are either once per week (for a weekend broadcast) or five times per week (for a Monday-Friday broadcast).

There are also standard lengths for shows in radio syndication.

First you must understand that there are two overall kinds of syndicated shows. The first is called "long form", meaning the show is 30 minutes or longer. The second is "short form", meaning the show runs 15 minutes or less.

Short Form Content

Let's look at short form content first.

Short form syndicated radio programs are usually scheduled on a Monday through Friday basis. These programs typically tell a quick story, give tips or advice, or share some interesting info or opinion.

Here are some typical, standard lengths for short form syndicated radio shows:

- 45 seconds
- 60 seconds
- 90 seconds
- 2 minutes
- 2.5 minutes
- 5 minutes (primarily for newscasts)

Of these, probably the most popular short form length is 60 seconds. Next in popularity would be 90 seconds, followed by 2 minutes. The 45 second shows are primarily designed to pair up with 15 second commercials.

General content (other than a newscast) that runs 2 minutes or longer will be more challenging to syndicate to commercial stations, especially those in larger markets.

Back in the old days, short form programs would sometimes run 10 to 15 minutes in length. Today, only one radio network we are aware of still offers a daily 15 minute news commentary in syndication. That quarter-hour length is mostly a relic of the past.

Short Form Commercial Placement

Short form programs are usually coupled with a 15, 30 or 60 second network commercial. The commercial either runs immediately after the program ("adjacent"), or as a "donut" (the program is produced with a mid-break, and the commercial runs in the middle).

The network commercials in your short form program belong to you. Stations agree to air your show, including the commercials, in exchange for your interesting and entertaining syndicated show. (Note: in traditional syndication, no cash changes hands. It is a barter or trade system. More about barter in an upcoming chapter.) As your network of stations grows more and more, the network commercials in your show can become quite valuable and can earn you a substantial income.

More about Commercials

In most cases, a 60 second short form program is followed by a 60 second commercial. This gives stations a neat two minute package that easily fits into their daily schedule. Likewise, a 90 second program can be coupled with a 30 second commercial, and this also results in a two minute package. A 45 second program can pair up with a 15 second ad, and this option only takes up one minute of airtime.

Stations will often sell a short form syndicated show to a local sponsor. Let's say your short form show is health oriented. The station must air it once with your network commercial, as agreed. Then they might sell additional airings of the show to a health related sponsor such as a local pharmacy. In that case, the show airs a second time, with the local spot replacing your network spot. This is perfectly fine, because your network commercial ran one time, as promised. Now the station gets to profit from your show as well, with a local sponsorship. Popular short form shows may air multiple times per day, on some stations, with many local sponsors attached.

Long Form Content

Now let's look at some standard lengths for **long form** radio shows:

- 30 minutes
- 1 hour
- 2 hours
- 3 hours
- 4 hours
- And longer

The weekend is a particularly popular time for stations to run long form syndication. A once-per-week talk show running 1, 2, or 3 hours long on the weekend is particularly well accepted.

But if your radio show is not one of these standard lengths, it falls into a "no man's land" for syndication. You will need to add or subtract content to create a show that conforms to one of the lengths listed above, to make it acceptable to radio stations.

Incidentally, the 30 minute show length may be less easy to sell to stations. This is because some stations may find it difficult to fit into their hourly schedule. Virtually all stations operate on an hourly clock schedule, so in order to air your 30 minute show they'll usually need to find another 30 minute show to pair with it, to fill out the hour.

Yet there are some successful 30 minute shows in syndication. That is why we include it on the list of accepted times. Just understand that this length may make it a little more challenging for some stations to accept your show.

Keep in mind that these standard length long form shows won't have to contain full hours of your own content, because commercials will fill a portion of the airtime.

Long Form Commercial Loads

Here's another way that podcasts differ from syndicated radio shows. Syndicated radio shows typically contain more commercials than do podcasts.

The average podcast may contain a pre-roll spot break, a mid-roll spot break, and a post-roll spot break – which adds up to around three to five minutes of ads in the typical podcast.

On the other hand, a syndicated talk show might contain 12 to 14 minutes of commercials per hour. The ads typically run in breaks lasting 3 or 4 minutes, in between segments of the show.

This is one reason why successful syndicated radio shows are more lucrative than podcasts: they contain more commercials. Generally speaking, radio listeners accept the fact that radio shows contain this many ads.

Usually, about half of the ad minutes in your syndicated show will belong to you the host, and the other half of the ad minutes are given to the local station, for local sale.

The number of minutes may vary depending on how you set up your show clock, but this is a typical formula.

Long Form Options

Because of the spot load, a one hour radio talk show needs at most 48 minutes of actual content, assuming it contains 12 minutes of spots (or 46 minutes of content, with 14 minutes of spots).

Less content than that is also acceptable, if you choose to leave a window at the top of the hour for the station to air a newscast. In that case, your show will actually begin at five minutes past the hour, so the total minutes you need to fill in the hour will be reduced by five more minutes. So in this example, one hour contains 12 minutes of spots + 5 minutes of news = 17 minutes, which leaves 43 minutes of show content you will create, per hour.

Recent research reveals that the average podcast has a running time of 35 minutes. If your podcasts run about this long, you'll only need to produce a few more minutes of additional content to fill a typical one-hour syndicated radio talk show.

As you can see from these examples, there is no exact, standard format for long form syndication. Different shows contain different spot loads. Some talk shows leave room at the beginning of each hour for hourly network news, some do not. Most stations will accept any of these variations, so the choices are really yours. But once you choose a format, structure, and show clock, you should stick with it.

We've included sample show clocks in the appendix of the book. Any one of these clock variations are accepted in radio syndication.

Choosing a Show Length

Now is the time to think carefully about the format of your syndicated radio show.

Should it be a 60 second daily feature or a 4 hour weekend show, or something in between? Will your show be heard every day, or once a week? Should you do both types of shows simultaneously: a short form vignette AND a long form show?

Don't assume you need to do a multi-hour show to achieve your goals. It is possible to make a reasonable income and create a national platform for success with only a 60 second daily feature, or with a one hour weekly show. Consider your needs, the anticipated workload, your ability to create fresh content, and the potential income, before locking in the length of your syndicated radio show.

A Few More Syndication Products

Just for the sake of completeness, we'll briefly mention a few more things that can be syndicated to radio stations. There are full-time formats, for example a 24/7 music service in a certain musical genre. Likewise, hourly news and weather reports are often provided to stations via syndication.

Other items that can be syndicated include service elements, such as imaging audio production, fully produced promos and commercials, and voiceover talent. Really, the options for syndication are only limited by market demand and the talent pool available to the syndicator.

Now let's turn to the next step to success in radio syndication.

Chapter Six

Get On the Air, Anywhere

Once you finalize your show content, length, and schedule, and produce at least one sample episode, you should prepare for regular, ongoing production of the show. But first you need to get it on the air, anywhere. We recommend getting your show on one radio station before you try to syndicate it nationally. Think about this as planting a seed to grow something. In other words, you have to start somewhere, or you're nowhere.

Brokered Airtime

The first question potential stations will probably ask is this: is your syndicated show on the air? If you reply "Not yet, we were hoping to syndicate it by starting with you", you won't be taken seriously. Few stations will want to touch a syndicated program that isn't on any stations. So how do you get on that first station? Well, there are two basic ways.

The first option is to buy the air time. In any market, large or small, there are stations that will be very happy to broadcast your show for a reasonable fee. But don't ask the top station in town, unless you have a big bank account. Call several of the less popular stations and ask if they sell brokered time. Tell them you have a syndicated show you'd like them to run. They will probably want to hear a sample episode of your show. Most stations will happily sell you a time slot for a reasonable fee, or even less in a small city or suburban market. Since you bought the air time, you own it. The station will air your show, and you can sell the ads in your show to offset the cost of air time.

From Guest to Host

Another way to get on that first station is to have a station give you the time. Radio is a people business, so if you're willing to make an effort to get to know the people at one of your local stations, you may be able to get your own time slot at no charge. One way to do this is to work your way in, by offering to be a guest expert on a show. Then, offer to fill in for on air people during vacations.

Another approach (which has launched the careers of several major market talk show hosts) is to be a regular caller to a talk station. This of course assumes that your comments are fairly entertaining and thought provoking, each time you call in to the station.

Any outstanding caller who has a good on-air personality will be welcomed whenever they phone a talk show, and will likely become popular with the host and the listeners. That can lead to an invitation to visit the station and to sit in on the show. In time, you can become a regular guest, and eventually a show host yourself.

In short, follow the path of some of today's well-known radio hosts: let the station staff get to know you, and you may end up with a show of your own.

If you launch a syndicated show in this way, be sure the station agrees up front to let you syndicate it. Some stations might claim your show belongs to them, if you didn't make it clear at the start that you own it. So we suggest before you syndicate your show, have the station sign a letter that says you own the concept and title of the show. This is easiest to do at the beginning, rather than later once your show has popularity and momentum.

"I'm thinking of stopping a podcast."

Internet Radio

What if you host an Internet radio show? A few years ago, taking an Internet radio show to national radio syndication would be unlikely. Internet radio was considered amateurish by many station executives.

But with the advent of semi-professional Internet radio shows that have mass appeal and good production values, this barrier has been lowered. Notice we said high quality and good production values. Your show must have the same high standards of sound quality, timing, and other factors we are discussing here as any professional radio show would.

If you host an Internet talk show over the phone, that will not sound professional. Your voice needs to be studio quality. The show intro and other elements need to be top notch. Just because some web site says you're a radio host, does not make you a professional. What's the solution? If you host a talk show, and you follow broadcast standards of format and structure (and there are several Internet talk show sites which conform to these standards), this can be a springboard to syndication.

Working with a Network or Syndicator

Another option to get on the air, anywhere is to partner with an established syndication company or network. This gives your show a mantle of authority from the start. Stations will assume your show is already established since it is represented by a professional syndicator. The syndication company will sign up stations to carry your show, handle distribution of your show, and once your show has established itself on a minimum number of stations, they can sell the ads in your show, earning you an income.

Chapter Seven

Your Demo and Branding

So now let's move to the next step in syndication success, and that is to create an audio demo and branding for your show, which will convince stations across the country to add your show. The main message here is simple: don't skimp on quality. Your demo and branding will be your ambassadors. Along with your audio demo, you'll want a one page sell sheet (details ahead). But just how important to success is your audio demo?

Importance of the Demo

When marketing your radio show to the broadcasting industry, you can describe it, write about it, explain it and demonstrate your excitement for it until you're blue in the face.

But nothing is more vital to get across the essence of your show to key radio decision makers than the audio demo. Virtually every program director will want to hear a sample of your show before they commit to put it on their station. There are rare exceptions to this rule, but unless you are already a famous household name, or your show is backed by a major media brand, even the most trusting program director or general manager will want to hear a sample of the show before signing up for it.

In the syndication business, we sometimes hear eager station executives say, "Oh, I'm sure it must be good if your company is involved, so go ahead and sign me up." But this occurs rarely and only if the syndicator has a very good reputation. Even so, it doesn't happen very often. Since radio executives are pitched on new shows all the time, they usually want to carefully check out a prospective show before signing up. And the first thing they ask for is the audio demo.

You might liken this process to tasting an orange for the first time. Think about it. How would you describe the taste of an orange to someone who has never eaten an orange? You could say it tastes something like a grapefruit but different. You could say it's juicy and delicious. You could even create new words like orangetastic or juice-o-rific. Marketers do that sometimes to give their product a unique marketing position.

When it comes to an orange, there are all sorts of adjectives you could use. But no matter how many words you use, it's no substitute for having someone take an actual taste of an orange. No matter how many ways you described it, they'd learn so much more from that first bite of the orange.

Likewise, station people want a taste of your show. So when you give that very first sample, you want it presented in the best way possible. As your mom used to say, "You never get a second chance to make a good first impression."

In terms of branding your show, here are some basic steps to take. Scope out any competitive shows and clearly differentiate your content from theirs. Have a talented designer create a graphic logo for your show. Create a positioning statement for your show that concisely says what it's all about. Then make sure your actual show content accurately reflects these branding elements.

Because the audio demo is so important, we'll devote an upcoming chapter to this, titled The Ingredients of a Killer Demo.

Marketing Your Show to Stations

One expensive mistake that beginners sometimes make is to physically send their demo on a CD to hundreds of stations that never asked for it in the first place. That's very wasteful since most stations will simply toss out the disc without even listening to it. It's also not very effective.

Since marketing requires repetition to be effective, you can't really pitch them with a one-time mailing. You have to pitch them repeatedly to get results. You want to reach stations over and over and over again with frequent reminders about your show.

You may assume that using the web and email to market your show to stations are the most effective ways to do it. But station executives are very busy people these days. Many of them have email filters and other roadblocks to avoid being buried by email pitches from show hosts like you.

We suggest doing something that few syndicators actually do: mail a basic one-page flyer or postcard to every station that might possibly carry your show.

Then several weeks later, mail it again, and then again, and again.

You can buy a database and do this yourself, or hire a promotional postcard company to do it for you. We liken this to water dripping on a rock, over time it can have a very significant effect. But again, just doing it once or twice won't be effective. Repetition is what makes it effective.

Creating Awareness

What other ways can you make stations aware of your show? Obviously, you can call stations directly. You can send out e-mails (the most common way to promote a show). You can buy ads on industry websites or in industry newsletters. You can send out press releases. You're only limited by your imagination here. More about email marketing in a moment, but first let's consider how to communicate your marketing message.

The Ideal Sell Sheet

The sell sheet (sometimes called the one sheet or the sales sheet) is the companion PDF marketing piece that supports the audio demo. Whatever you call this PDF, there are five things you must put on that PDF. Here's what those five things are.

Sell Sheet Key No. 1 - Show Name and Host Name

First, and most obvious, include the name of the show and the host's name. If your show has a graphic logo – and we suggest it should – that takes care of the name of the show (just make sure your logo is easy to read!) Then, add the host's name. For example, centered at the top of the page it might say: [SHOW LOGO] with Dr. Susan Smith.

If you have a great photo of yourself, fit that into the page near the top. You might put the host name under the photo.

Sell Sheet Key No. 2 - Slogan, Bullet Points

Beneath the logo and host name, put a slogan (otherwise called a sub-headline or positioning statement). For example: "Healthy Talk from a Trusted Medical Expert".

Below that, list several bullet points that describe the show and why it is great. This is where your carefully crafted marketing messages come in.

Sell Sheet Key No. 3 - Length of the Show

The third key is the length of the show. Don't assume anybody knows this. Is your show 60 seconds daily, or 3 hours on the weekend? Don't make them guess, tell them.

Sell Sheet Key No. 4 - Terms of the Deal

The fourth thing – the business terms of the show. In other words, is it available on barter or for cash? If barter (like most syndicated shows), how many minutes of barter commercials per episode or per hour?

Sell Sheet Key No. 5 - Show Distribution Details

And fifth – how does the station get the show? Do they receive it by satellite or Internet download or another way? This point alone may determine whether a station can carry it or not.

Your Contact Information

If you skip any of these five ingredients, you will have prospects scratching their heads wondering about the missing things they need to know. Your sales sheet will either end up in the trash or in the slush pile, with all the other unimportant material at the far corner of the desk.

Last but not least, make sure you include your phone number, email, website address and so on at the very bottom of the PDF. This makes it easy for the station to contact you to sign up or get more information.

In designing the sell sheet, leave some white space and don't pack the page with words and pictures. If there's too much text, some PDs may not bother to even read it.

Marketing via Email

With just a few modifications your sell sheet info can be used as an email blast to radio stations.

We do not recommend emailing stations an audio demo or emailing them the PDF as an attachment (unless requested to do so). Corporate email systems may reject emails with unknown files attached. Even if the email gets through, station executives may hesitate to open a file they weren't expecting to get.

So it's best to create an attractive email with nice (but minimal) graphics.

The email should include links to hear the demo, to download the PDF sell sheet, and to download an agreement to sign up for the show.

All the rules of good email marketing apply. The last thing you want is to be seen as a spammer sending junk mail. We recommend sending your email blasts through an established Email Service Provider (ESP) for best results.

Take the time to verify everything in your email is correct. Make sure to carefully proofread it for spelling and punctuation errors before hitting the send button.

The Worst Email Errors

Now on to our list of the eight worst email errors. You definitely want to avoid these mistakes like the plague, or all your time and hard work will go down the drain.

Mistake No. 1 - Not Telling Them What to Do

Give your prospects a **clear action step** to follow, such as, "Go to this web address now to sign up" or "Call this number now" or "Click here to learn more" or "Reply to this email now."

Mistake No. 2 - Not Including Any Graphics

The second mistake is not using graphics that please the eye. Email needs to go beyond pure text. **Add a few graphics** or photos to capture their imagination.

Mistake No. 3 - Not Targeting by Station Format

The third boo-boo is not thinking about the **format of stations** you're targeting. If you do a Country music show, email to Country stations, not urban or talk stations.

Mistake No. 4 - Not Having a Way to Opt-out

Unwanted email can be annoying, so include a line that tells them **how to unsubscribe**.

Mistake No. 5 - Not Specifying the Recipient

Since you're pitching syndication, **target the program director**. So you might say "Attention: Program Director" or if you have actual recipient names, even better!

Mistake No. 6 - Overloading Their Mailbox

This is about timing. A well-written email is generally accepted by stations. But sending another email right away with the same message, or sending emails over and over, can get annoying.

Mistake No. 7 - Not Editing Your Message

This is about saying too much. **The fewer words, the better**. Boil it down to the most powerful, succinct message possible. Keep it simple. Leave white space on the page.

Mistake No. 8 - Not Choosing the Best Time for Delivery

The **day and time you send** an email can make a big difference. Some experts say Tuesday morning is a good time to send business email. See what works for you.

Avoid these eight mistakes in sending your marketing messages to stations and you will be ahead of the competition.

Chapter Eight

Signing Up Stations

The next step in successful syndication is convincing lots of stations to carry your show.

It's a fact that any syndicated show is only as good as its list of affiliate stations. As your marketing goes out to stations, calls may come in. Most callers probably won't sign up on the spot, but they will want follow-up details. And then it may require you to make one or more follow up calls to get them to send back the agreement to carry your show. Usually, multiple phone calls and a little persistence are needed from you (or your syndicator) to convince these interested stations to sign up and carry your show.

Get Past Gatekeepers

One problem that often happens when calling stations is you end up with those wonderful gatekeepers, the people whose job it is to intercept calls like yours and keep you from bothering the decision makers. This one subject could easily fill an entire book. But here is one simple tip. Try calling very early or very late in the business day. Sometimes the person you wish to talk to will pick up the phone themselves at these times.

You'd be surprised how well this approach works in radio, since the number of people working at stations is fewer than it used to be.

Pitch Both High and Low

If you can't reach the program manager or group programmer, why not go to the top of the company? While the top person may only respond with the name of someone in the chain of command who will decide to take your show, a side benefit is you begin to build a relationship with the head honcho. Relationships matter in broadcasting, so never be afraid to go to the top.

The reverse is also true. Someone at the bottom may prove especially helpful. Most radio people in middle management are very busy. But there may be an intern or an assistant that will take your call or answer your email. They may have time to look over your materials and perhaps bring them directly to the attention of the decision maker.

Tips for Voicemail

Often you'll end up in station voicemail. How can you get stations to call you back? One tried and true method is to say you have info to share about something they may want to know. This might be activity you heard about that's happening in their market. Don't spill the beans on voicemail. Make them call you back for that juicy piece of info.

You can also offer a freebie gift if they call back, assuming you have some marketing goodies to give away. You might briefly explain how your show will get them ratings and make them money, then ask for a call back. Whatever your message, your voicemails will be more powerful if you give your phone number at the beginning and at the end of the message. Don't make them search for your number. And don't meander around or leave a boring message they must wade through. Get right to the point and get off the phone.

Closing the Deal

In the sales game, the last part of the selling process is called the close. Remember, all your hard work doesn't pay off until the deal closes, when the station signs on the bottom line and agrees to carry your show. If you choose to handle the affiliate relations process yourself, be prepared for some rejection.

Think about rejection this way. There are over 10,000 full time commercial radio stations in the US. Depending on the type of show you do, there may be several thousand stations in the US that could be good prospects to carry your show. Big success in syndication typically means getting 100 or more stations to broadcast your show. So it's clear that anyone who calls stations to pitch a syndicated show is going to hear lots of NO's before they hear a YES. But with time and persistence, a quality show can build a big list of affiliates. Rejection is just part of the process of getting to the promised land.

Major market stations are more challenging to sign up, but even this can be done with real persistence and a personal touch. As we've mentioned, there are also syndication companies and networks that will handle the process for you. You may also outsource this work to a freelancer, but we advise you to first review their track record. Ask to see testimonials from other hosts they've worked with. You don't want to put the all-important station sales process in the hands of the wrong person, as that may tarnish your show's reputation if they're too aggressive or too amateurish in how they contact stations.

Advice on Outsourcing

If you get an unsolicited call or email from someone wanting to represent your show, here's some advice. Before you consider handing over the all-important marketing process for your show to some unknown person, ask yourself a question. If this person is really that good in a field as competitive as broadcast syndication, why do they need to cold call or send out emails to find new clients? Unfortunately, there are some flaky folks who pitch themselves to unsuspecting show hosts. So, check out a prospective marketing agent before you commit.

This rule holds true for any product or service. If you get an unsolicited call or email from somebody trying to sell you something, learn more about them before making a commitment. Don't make a decision based solely on a slick looking website or a smooth sounding voice.

So what's the final step? You're on the air. Your show is on stations. What's left? The next chapter has the answer.

Chapter Nine

Take Care of Business

The final key to the **Six Steps to Successful Syndication** is an important and ongoing process. "TCB" includes selling commercials in your show, producing your episodes in a consistently entertaining, quality manner, and distributing the show to stations. Like most things in life, all these things are fairly easy to accomplish once you know how.

Selling Commercials

There is a process to syndication ad sales. In upcoming chapters, we'll share strategies to sell broadcast radio show ads, as we are most often asked about this process. Understand that selling the ads in your syndicated radio show is a multistep effort. It will take a little prep time to follow the steps we're going to share. Of course, it's always possible that a deal might instantly fall into your lap from a potential advertiser, and they'll want to buy ads on the spot, but you really can't count on that happening.

There are syndicated show hosts who do very well hosting their show and selling the commercials too. This is possible for you, too. It simply will take more time than simply hosting the show. You may be thinking "I'm not a sales person, I don't know how to sell". No worries, the process we're going to describe will be easily accomplished by just about anyone.

You might recall earlier in the book I mentioned some highly successful and well established syndicated shows. Keep in mind, these shows started in the same place as you are – with zero income. If they were able to achieve financial success with their show, so can you. You just need to learn the steps involved in ad sales, and follow through.

As we said, there's a certain amount of prep work needed before you'll be ready to sell ads in the show. Don't think it's going to be incredibly difficult, because it's not. In fact, the preliminary steps are all pretty basic. In our opinion, it's much better for you to take care of these important prep steps first, rather than risk blowing it with a potential advertiser, by trying to sell ads before you have your sales act together.

We'll get to those exact steps in the pages ahead. But there is one thing you can do first to maximize sales later.

Plan Now to Get Maximum Income

If you're still in the planning stages of taking your podcast to syndicated radio broadcast, there is something to consider which may boost your eventual income. Let's jump into this right now.

We previously discussed choosing a relatively broad show topic for syndication. But going too wide with the show topic can make it less easy for you to sell to advertisers. You must strike the right balance between wide and narrow.

One factor for sales success in syndication is the idea of owning a key niche topic with your show. If your show focuses on a specific topic or concept, it's often the case that you can boost your ad sales by making sure the focus of your show is carefully tuned. This will make it easier to attract advertisers who wish to reach that specific niche audience.

The Right Niche Means Money

Let's say your podcast is about business. And now you want to do a syndicated radio talk show about business. If you can narrow your radio show to one aspect of business, that may help you sell more ads, because you will offer advertisers a more targeted audience.

For example, you could focus on the topic of small business, which is narrower and more focused than business in general. And there are lots of advertising dollars chasing those with small businesses.

How about niching it even more tightly? For example, let's say you focused your show on female-owned small business. If that is legitimately your primary area of expertise -- assuming you're a woman and you own a small business -- even better! You will speak from a position of authority, and advertisers will make the obvious connection. It will be easy for them to recognize you as an expert on the topic of your show, which is female small business. You have real credibility. Assuming you have a decent sized audience, ad buyers wishing to target female small business owners will accept your show as a good vehicle for their ad campaign.

However, if you're a female small business owner, and you've decided to do a general talk show about all aspects of business, that's fine too. Just don't expect advertisers to seek you out as a general business expert, because there are many others already doing shows in the same realm of general business. Thus you'll be competing for advertisers among all other general business shows in syndication. This is why we suggest niching your show topic a bit, and focusing the content if possible, to make your show more unique and sellable.

Let's look at another example. Consider a tightly niched show in this category, a show titled *The Home Office Hour*. As we're sure you know, home offices are a sub, sub genre of business and a sub genre of small business. The Home Office radio show was designed to be a weekly, one-hour radio talk show about the ins and outs of working from a home office. The name explains it all.

This show quickly captured the attention of advertisers who were interested in targeting this narrow customer niche with specific products and services those advertisers want to sell. Not only that, but companies freely sent the host free samples of products designed for home offices, in hopes of getting mentioned during the show.

We'll describe the full step by step process for selling ads in a later chapter.

Distributing Your Show to Stations

The final part of Taking Care of Business is getting your show to stations, otherwise known as show distribution. If your radio show is recorded (not fed to stations live), that simplifies the process greatly. You simply provide the audio file of your show to stations, so they can download it before the actual broadcast date.

It's best to give stations a two-day lead time. So for example if you do a weekend radio show, you would post the recorded episodes for download no later than the preceding Thursdays.

The most basic way to do this is to post the shows on a download site (such as Dropbox), on a page of your web site, or on a password-protected FTP site. Then tell your stations to visit the appropriate place to download your show.

There are also companies that specialize in the delivery of radio shows to stations, including Radio Spider, Mr. Master and Synchronicity.

If you host a short form daily show, it's best to post an entire week's worth of shows (one episode per day, Monday through Friday) on your download site, or in an email to your stations, no later than the preceding Thursday. Stations need a day or two to download your shows and input them to their system for later broadcast.

Hosting a Live Syndicated Show

If you plan to host a live syndicated radio show (such as a caller-driven live talk show) this will add complexity and expense to the distribution.

Think carefully about your goals and needs before choosing to do a live radio broadcast. A live show requires you (or another host) to always be sitting in the "air chair" every weekday or every weekend, at the appointed air time. You will likely need help from a call screener, producer or engineer to assist you during the live show. Live syndicated shows usually involve a commercial satellite provider or a special type of enhanced web connection. It is not considered professional to use a consumer web streaming site such as YouTube to feed a live radio show to stations, due to buffering and bandwidth issues.

If you choose to go live using a satellite, feeding your live show audio to the satellite uplink requires purchase of a codec unit and other studio gear, plus a high speed Internet connection.

Again, while a number of live web stream providers (such as YouTube, Twitch, and Facebook) make it easy to go live on the web, few radio stations will accept a live feed from one of these platforms.

They prefer a professional satellite feed which interfaces with their station system for automated live program switching or later playback.

Here's something else to consider. Let's say you decide to host a live talk show every Saturday morning from 8am to 10am Eastern Time. There is no guarantee you will actually get live station clearances in that time slot. Some stations may choose to record your live show as it is fed, and broadcast it at a less popular time, such as early evening or late night. This means your live show will never be heard live on that station.

But if your heart is set on doing a live syndicated radio show, it is certainly possible to do so. There are various ways to accomplish this goal. Talk to some established syndicators and satellite providers. Research the process, then choose the best technical and staffing approach for your particular needs and budget.

Review the Steps

Let's review the **Six Steps to Successful Syndication**:

- Content Creation
- Format for Syndication
- Get On the Air, Anywhere
- Demo and Branding
- Signing Up Stations
- Take Care of Business

Follow these steps as many others have, and you will soon be on the road to success with your syndicated show.

Chapter Ten

Marketing Mindset

We already touched on marketing your syndicated show to radio stations. This outreach is a vital and important part of syndication and this chapter will expand on it.

Foundation of Marketing

As we begin, the first thing to consider may seem somewhat abstract, but we assure you it's going to be the foundation for all your marketing efforts. You must consider your state of mind and your level of focus, enthusiasm and energy about your show. If you have an attitude of complete determination and total belief that your show will be a huge success, that's the mental rocket fuel that's going to carry you past all the naysayers and doomsday thinkers who you will no doubt encounter during your quest for growth in syndication.

Think about marketing this way: marketing literally puts life energy into your show. The human body acquires much of its life energy by eating food. To stay healthy, most experts agree that every human should eat three meals a day, every day, every week, every year of their life. One meal alone won't do it. You have to feed your hunger on an ongoing basis. Likewise, marketing cannot be a one-shot effort if you want your syndication business to grow and thrive. It has to be a daily, weekly, monthly and yearly effort that's never-ending. This doesn't mean you have to spend money every day, but it does mean you have to keep your mind attuned to marketing opportunities and ideas on a constant basis and just as important, follow through on those opportunities and ideas.

We'll get into low-cost and no-cost ways to do this later in the chapter. There are many syndication marketing approaches that require little or no expenditure other than a little time and effort. But understand, the way you think about marketing is all-important. Make it a priority to devote yourself to marketing your show. Then keep reminding yourself to do it and follow through using phone memos, post-it notes, calendars or whatever works for you. Do this and you'll have built a sound foundation for results once you understand and apply the marketing ideas we are going to share here.

The Customer's Point of View

There's a saying about dating: "If all you do on the first date is talk about yourself, there won't be a second date."

This reflects a key aspect of the marketing mindset – seeing things from your customer's point of view. For example, you might think the best thing about your syndicated radio show is that it's produced in high definition, quadraphonic, Dolby, THX surround sound, but the radio executive considering your show for an AM radio station, which in most cases broadcasts in glorious mono, couldn't care less about that fact. They might want a show like yours for a completely different reason.

Now this example is a little farfetched, but the point is many syndicators completely miss the one or two key marketing points that will make their prospects sit up and take notice, and consider adding the show to their station.

Consider these famous facts about how some others discovered their best marketing points. Charles Revson, who founded the makeup company Revlon, one day realized his company wasn't selling beauty products; it was actually selling hope – hope for a better appearance, a better relationship and so on. By marketing with that angle, Revlon sales grew far faster. Disney World didn't just market itself as a fun place to spend a vacation, but as the best way for you to bond more closely with your family.

Notice in each of these examples – Revlon and Walt Disney World – the businesses figured out their customers' deepest reason for purchasing. Also notice that each of these companies found a connection between the product or service and an emotional feeling or deeply felt need of their customer. If you can do this, it will have fairly powerful results. Try to figure out the underlying emotional hook of your potential customer. We'll explore this approach more and how it applies to syndication in the pages ahead.

Consider Your Marketing Options

So what are your options when it comes to marketing your show to the industry? For those who are observant and intelligent, the modern world we live in is a literal school of higher education in marketing. If you watch TV, listen to the radio, look at billboards and magazine ads and online ads, if you get junk postal mail and spam email, or if you use a search engine on the Internet – really the list is endless – well, each of these contain marketing messages. If you're like most people, you probably do all you can to tune out this constant barrage of advertising and marketing.

But now I want you to think about the marketing that has really worked well, marketing that broke through the barriers, marketing that caused you to take notice or take action or that sent you in a certain direction or marketing that is simply stuck in your brain. To do this exercise properly, you might want to do a little brainstorming so grab a pen. Below on this page there is space for you to jot down a few words about the different ads, slogans, images or concepts that you've seen repeatedly and that you can recall in some way.

Now it doesn't have to have anything to do with radio syndication or your syndicated show. It might be an ad or marketing message or slogan for any product or service, maybe even one you would never use, but if you've seen a particular marketing message repeatedly and it's managed to stick in your head, then there's a lesson to be learned. That particular message has somehow managed to get past all your mental filters and attempts to ignore it and it has penetrated your brain. Of course, that's the goal of all marketing, to be remembered by the prospective customer, especially at the key moment of decision-making. If you want to do this little exercise, now is the time to do so.

LIST SOME MEMORABLE MARKETING MESSAGES:

_____

_____

_____

_____

_____

_____

_____

Why Some Marketing Messages Stick

Now if you followed through with that exercise, congratulations. If you didn't, we hope you'll do it later. It's a fascinating thing when you take a mental snapshot of the marketing that is top of mind for you on this particular day in your life. If you came back and did this same exercise a year from now some of the products or slogans you recall would be the same; others would be different. And this should tell you two things. First, the marketing messages that would be different, those messages penetrated your consciousness on a fairly recent and superficial basis. They're lodged in your short-term memory.

On the other hand, some messages might be the same a year from now. Those are embedded in your long-term memory. These persistent, long-term messages are the real winners in the battle for space in your brain. In many cases, they may be messages from very successful companies. These marketers are reaping the result of consistent marketing efforts. Perhaps they aren't actively marketing right now, but if their message is stuck in your brain long term, we'd bet they made a long-term investment at some time in the past in order for you to recall them so readily.

Ongoing Marketing is Best

That's one reason why a commitment to ongoing marketing is the best strategy. Naturally, it gives you the best ongoing results. The fact is you just don't know when the need is going to come along for your syndicated show at a particular station. For example, a station may be changing format or a new program director may be taking charge of a station. Or a general manager may be looking for syndication as a sales vehicle or to reduce the bottom-line cost of programming.

You cannot know or predict when these sorts of decision points will occur at each of the thousand or more of different stations that are most likely to add your show. That's why ongoing marketing is best. It vastly increases the odds that your message will be remembered by the decision makers, at the moment you need to be remembered.

What's <u>Your</u> Message?

This brings us to a very important consideration. What is your marketing message? It's worth the time to think this through before you invest much time or money in actual marketing. Start by asking yourself a few key questions. First, what are your qualifications to do your show? Do you have the credentials or at the very least the passion and interest in the topic to carry it through successfully on the air?

Keep in mind, some of today's most successful syndicated show hosts had few credentials aside from a burning passion to communicate their interest with listeners. You don't necessarily need a degree or years of experience in a field, but it doesn't hurt either.

MY MESSAGE IS:

_____

_____

_____

_____

What Are Your Goals?

Another question to ask yourself: what are your goals in doing the show? Is it to be the best at doing a show? Is it to make money? Is it to gain recognition for your name and business? Or all of these and more?

Think about it and then list your goals, in any order you wish.

MY GOALS ARE:

_____

_____

_____

_____

_____

Who's Your Target?

Third, what is your target audience? In other words, which segment of the entire national radio audience will be most interested in your show? If you say "everyone", that's not realistic. You have to focus in on specifics.

Determine your primary audience: male or female, their age range, income level, educational level and so on. Is that audience potentially big enough to support and sustain your show? Is it an audience that you think some advertisers would find attractive? Is it an audience you can easily reach through national radio? Think about this and answer these questions.

MY TARGET AUDIENCE:

_____

_____

_____

_____

Speaking of your target audience, can you guess how interested they will be in hearing your show? Ask yourself what other options your potential listeners already have, to hear a show like yours. Can you clearly picture your show carving out a successful niche? Chances are, if your show is somewhat different and you avoid a copycat approach, there'll be plenty of listeners available to you. But it's good to consider this point.

MY COMPETITION:

_____

_____

_____

_____

What Makes Your Show Unique?

And finally, what sets your show apart? What makes it unique, special and better than the competition? What competitive advantage do you provide listeners over similar shows? The more benefits your show offers to stations and listeners, the better it will do. Remember, your show must appeal to advertisers as well as listeners. Local stations will want to sell their own ads in and around your show, so if your show has advertiser appeal, that's a big plus. For example, a show on automobile maintenance and repair will attract listeners and at the same time, it will interest car-related advertisers who want to sponsor such a show.

WHAT SETS MY SHOW APART? HOW IS IT UNIQUE?

_____

_____

_____

_____

_____

So there you have a list of questions that will help you find your best marketing message. Answering these questions will reveal the recipe to forge a powerful message. The right message will help you blast through the walls of indifferent and entrenched thinking and get your show added to radio stations. In the wonderful world of marketing, perception is indeed reality. Create a powerful message that positions your show just right, and then back that message up with a well-produced program, and you have a winning combination for successful syndication.

If you haven't already done so, take the time to find the right recipe. Likewise, get to know your niche segment like the back of your hand. Find out all you can about your competition. Talk to listeners and potential listeners. When you notice their passion about something,, that's important information. Your success will happen when your show reaches listeners on that same emotional level. They'll tell others to listen, and these loyal, involved listeners will help you reach your goals.

Check Out Your Competition

As we've already suggested, listen to shows that delve into some of the same topics as yours does. While it is human nature to disparage the competition, be objective and ask yourself what they're doing right that you could do even better? What are their weaknesses and strengths? How can your show be more original, fresher and better?

If possible, talk to a few station executives. Ask for their opinions and advice. Listen carefully and absorb the nuggets of wisdom they share with you, and thank them for their time.

Working with a Syndicator

If you choose to work with a syndication company or network, understand they have experience in the business, possibly decades of experience. Let them guide you.

If you're lucky enough to find a good syndicator and then you try second-guessing them, telling them how you think everything needs to be done, then you're probably wasting your time and money.

There's an old saying in business: "Teamwork makes the dream work". In most cases you will find that teaming up with an established syndicator will accelerate your results and lower your stress level. Everything will get done the right way and on time -- not just by you.

What Do You Do?

As we've explained, if you choose to go solo in marketing your show to stations, you need to craft a marketing message that will position your show just right in the minds of station decision-makers. Well, here's something to consider.

Ask just about anyone you meet what they do for a living, and listen to their answer. Most will either stumble over their words, or they'll give a totally bland answer.

Why is this? It's simple. They haven't thought through their personal marketing message. Most people have never crafted a powerful, memorable statement that describes what they do for a living.

If right now someone walked up to you and asked, "What do you do?" what would be your immediate answer? Would your reply be bland or, even worse, confusing?

Let's say you work in finance and you're a financial planner. When asked what you do for a living, you might say, "I'm a financial planner." But that answer might make many people's eyes glaze over. It sounds very generic.

Instead, think about how most people see money. It's a tool to make things happen, and most people wish they had more of it! Knowing this, you might instead say, "I help people get rich so they can fulfill their ultimate goals and fantasies." Now saying this would capture people's attention, much more so than a generic, bland answer. They'd want to know more about you, and some might even want to become your clients. In any case, it sure sounds more exciting than saying you're a financial planner.

Apply this same rule to your syndicated radio show. Think about the specific benefits your show delivers and what aspects of it might deeply touch the passions of your audience. Then include this in a short statement that describes your show. This will probably take some effort. We didn't say this would be easy. But if you do it right, it will help you more rapidly climb the ladder of syndication success.

The Product Ladder

Speaking of ladders – and wasn't that a smooth segue? – let's briefly talk about a marketing concept called the product ladder. If you've never heard the term, it's easy to explain. In each person's mind, that person has a personal ranking of each brand name by category. Each product or brand name can be thought of as occupying a rung on the ladder.

So if we asked you to name some fast food chains, there'd probably be several rungs in your mental product ladder for those. A typical product ladder might include McDonald's, Wendy's, Burger King, Chick-fil-a, Popeye's and several more. You might put McDonald's on the top rung and, sure enough, they happen to be the number one fast food chain. In this case, perception is reality.

Your syndicated radio show must appear somewhere on the product ladder in the prospect's mind before they'll even consider adding it to their station.

Let's say you host a political talk show. There are other political talk shows out there and you can probably think of some right off the bat. Well, so can the station decision-maker. If they're not even aware of your show, they probably won't consider it. And when it comes time for that executive to choose a political talk show, will he or she choose your show, or some other one? This is where your show's rank on the product ladder comes in.

"A SURE-WIN RADIO TALK SHOW. PEOPLE PHONE IN WITH QUESTIONS ON EXISTENCE AND REALITY, AND YOU RESPOND WITH TOTAL SILENCE."

You earn a place on the product ladder for a specific niche show, such as political talk, by having a marketing message that's focused and effective, and by making your show the best it can be. But how do you get to a higher rung on the prospect's product ladder if his or her mental filters won't allow you to go to a higher rung?

For example, let's say you decide to compete directly against the leading political talk show host. You decide to imitate everything he does. Being a clone of the top guy will probably get you known, and you may get on the political talk show product ladder. But the top talker will always be above you. That's because any PD in their right mind will see you as nothing more than a copycat, a clone with a derivative show. The PD's mental mindset will keep you trapped on that lower rung.

Positioning Your Show

On the other hand, let's say you position your show in a very unique way as having some very special attributes and benefits. This information will help break through the mental filter and get prospective stations to look at your show in a different way. Depending on how unique your show is, it might even earn its own unique product ladder in your prospect's mind.

Now to use the political talk show example again, let's say you choose to specialize in targeting female libertarian listeners. That's the focus of your show. If your show is done right and it's also skillfully marketed, it would earn the attention of program directors.

Since the show would stand out so noticeably, it would earn a rung on the political talk show ladder. That's because who can think of any other female-skewing, libertarian talk show on radio? Well, you'd certainly earn the top rung on our product ladder for female libertarian radio shows.

In other words, if you're unique enough, you break through and create your very own category. This is just an example of how this works. The actual topic of your show has to be unique and noticeably different to earn you a higher rung on whatever product ladder you choose to be on, but it also has to have sufficient mass appeal for national radio.

By now you may have noticed something about constructing a solid marketing effort. If you're doing it right, it's forcing you to think very deeply about things you may never have considered -- such as the focus of your show, who it will most appeal to, the benefits it offers the audience, and how it will best serve radio stations that carry it.

What makes your show unique, fresh and different, separating it from all the others? And of course, you must consider your unique qualifications as a host and/or producer of the show. Are there ways you can enhance your reputation as a thought leader or expert?

If you want to have an effective marketing campaign, you first have to put in some serious thought. Sharpen the focus of every aspect of your brand. Ask yourself what your show is really about, why it's good and how it will evoke a response from listeners.

We strongly suggest you get these key points down on paper. Make sure you're comfortable with those answers, because they're going to guide many of your decisions ahead. If you plan to invest money to support your marketing effort, it may be wasted if you don't do the homework first and get your mission details nailed down.

So from this point forward, we are going to assume you have honed a relatively well thought out marketing message and a positioning statement for your show. It doesn't have to be Einstein's Theory of Relativity, just as long as your message is memorable and accurate. Make sure it sells the show to radio stations that might consider adding it.

This book is not meant to be a general course in marketing and advertising. There are many resources for that information. You might consider working with a PR professional who understands radio, to help you focus your message. Don't get hung up on having the most perfect marketing approach ever created. Just put in the effort to come up with a plan that feels solid and makes sense.

What to Never Say in Your Marketing

One thing we recommend never saying in your marketing is that your show is "brand new" to syndication, even if it is new. This may sound counterintuitive. Marketers of most products will tell you the word "new" is very positive. In fact, you see it plastered on nearly every package at the store. But in the world of radio syndication, we have found the word "new" means something very different to radio station executives. It means unproven and risky. So just don't use the word "new". Simply present your show as it is, without mentioning in your marketing material that you are new to the world of syndication.

The Life of a Radio Program Director

We can tell you from personal experience, being a radio program director can be stressful. One reason for this is the continuous pressure to increase the station's audience numbers, primarily within the target demographic of the station's format. For a PD, the next rating book may determine whether they get a raise or end up in the unemployment line. Aside from ratings, another stress producer is radio's constant 24 hour, 7 day nature. Much can happen during one day's news cycle. Important decisions may need to be made, often under time pressure.

A program director never knows if the phone will ring or an email will arrive with a last-minute crisis or a problem demanding an instant solution. Some radio groups have multiple managers which results in overlapping decision making. This can be a pitfall for a program director who isn't politically savvy. Owners, managers, consultants and (of course) listeners tell the PD how things should be done and when they should be done, usually right away.

Meanwhile, the program director has their own unique vision of how the station should sound, and they work to implement this vision within the radio station.

Now here you come with your syndicated radio program, approaching this very busy and often stressed-out key decision maker known as the program director. You want to know if he or she will add your show to the station. Understanding all of what we've just said about the world in which the average PD exists, you can see that the last thing they want is to add more risk to their life. Most PDs are already skilled tightrope walkers who are used to minimizing and avoiding risky choices.

To survive and thrive, their radar operates at all times, alert to avoid missteps or errors in decisions. One big blunder (or several small blunders) could put that PD out of a job. Program directors aren't people who love to take chances with unknown, new programs.

What to Do If You are New?

So what do you say if your show is new? You now know that the best way to present your show to a PD is not to position it as new, out-of-the-box, unproven or in its first month of broadcast. Nor that you've never been inside the door of a radio station – just the opposite!

PDs want syndicated shows that are proven winners, not shows that are of unknown origin. They want show hosts who are talented radio pros.

You want to be on the air at a station. In a manner of speaking, you're asking the PD to hire your show for their station. Few companies will hire an employee who has no track record, no references and no past successes in a particular field of expertise. So aside from avoiding the word "new," as we've mentioned, you should present your show in as reassuring a manner as possible to skeptical PDs who may never have heard of it. One obvious way to do this is to get a few testimonial comments from friendly program directors at other stations, and feature those remarks on your marketing material.

Another way is to have a reputable syndication company or network represent your show. Of course, your show has to be of good quality to begin with, or no reputable syndicator will be interested in representing it.

One more way to build credibility is to include station call letters in your marketing. You can legitimately do this if you have been interviewed as a guest expert on those stations.

Never been interviewed on radio? It's relatively easy to arrange, assuming you have some know-how in any area of expertise. You can contact show hosts or producers, suggesting you be a guest. Or you might have a PR person or a publicist set up some phone interviews with you on stations around the country. You do the interviews and now you can legitimately put these call letters in your marketing, as stations on which you've been heard. For program directors, just seeing that you've been on the air at a number of stations adds to your credibility and their comfort level.

If you've followed through on creating a solid marketing message, while avoiding common mistakes, you're moving right along. But if you skipped over these important choices, now's the time to go back and get those thoughts in writing.

Chapter Eleven

The Ingredients of a Killer Demo

In this chapter we're going to cover the key ingredients of your audio demo. Then we'll give you some tips for the proper length, pacing, content and so on. After that, we'll explore some ways you can deliver that demo to your kcy station prospects.

There are five key ingredients to any effective demo. Here they are.

Killer Ingredient No. 1 - High Production Values

Number one, your demo must be highly produced. A demo that mostly contains someone's dry voice droning on and on is boring! That is not the way to sell your show to a radio executive who probably has a very short attention span. You want to create excitement from the start. Even if you're an undertaker and you host a talk show about funeral planning, your demo must have energy and sizzle from the moment it begins.

How do you make a demo highly produced? Well, a talented audio production person can easily come up with ways to make that happen, but here are some suggestions.

- Begin the demo with a bang, with sounds or statements that catch the ear.

- Make the demo fast-paced. Keep it moving.

- Make the content interesting with good scripting and delivery.

- Use music, at least under any announcer bits or transitions.

- Don't be afraid to push the envelope with the music. It can be hard and edgy.

- Keep the audio changing constantly. Use multiple voices.

You can use sound effects or production elements as punctuators or stingers, but don't overdo these.

Your goal is to have a rich, textured, fascinating demo. That's what "highly produced" means.

Killer Ingredient No. 2 - Start with an Audio Montage

Here's the second ingredient. Begin the demo with an audio montage of some type, either a montage of people saying how great your show it or a montage of the best moments of your show, or some variation of this. A cascading array of sound clips is powerful, when it's done right.

Now you may have noticed something about the first and second points here. We are not suggesting that your demo simply contain a straight, unedited example of your show with no elaboration. That will not be very effective, yet that's what many demos contain.

The goal is to set up the listener, to pre-sell them on your show before they actually hear a full sample of it. So you might start the demo with a professional voiceover talent and well-written script, interspersed with an audio montage of voices or show bits.

This initial montage of sound clips should run no longer than a minute or two, and definitely no more than two minutes. That's a long time, by radio demo standards.

At that point, the listener should be primed and ready to hear a full sample show. If the initial pre-sell portion of the demo has done its job, the station executive already feels positive about you. Now it's time to close the deal with a solid show sample. You don't want to let them down at this point.

Killer Ingredient No. 3 - A Great Show Sample

Obviously, a great sample show is the third key ingredient of your demo. Now just as you wouldn't mail someone a job resume that contains misspellings, smudged ink and other mistakes, likewise your show sample should sound as perfect as it can be. It should not contain audio glitches, clicks, hum, buzzing or other flaws. And of course the host's performance should be as good as possible.

The show sample you choose should reflect the optimum content of the show. When the station executive hears your demo, that's when they will imagine how it would sound on their station. Don't hide your best stuff one minute into the sample show. Put it right at the top. Or to describe it another way, skip the salad and the main course, and go straight to the dessert.

We've seen station executives impatiently listen to the first 30 seconds of a sample show waiting to hear something great, but rejecting it, simply because it sounded boring to their ears. They didn't want to wait around for it to get better.

This is why it's critical to start with an energetic pre-sell (see points 1 and 2 above), and then hit them with your best shot -- a great show sample.

If you host a long form show that runs an hour or longer, then your montage might contain best bits extracted from your show. Follow that montage with a full one hour episode, minus any commercials.

Sometimes, a demo only contains a sampling of bits. But most savvy program directors will want to hear a full episode, before they commit. That's why we suggest including one full episode on your demo.

If your syndicated show is short form – in other words, if episodes are under two minutes (such as a short feature vignette or info tip) -- you'll want to put several samples on the demo. Three episodes is a good number.

Killer Ingredient No. 4 - Add a Strong Close

Here's the fourth ingredient of a great demo. It comes after the show sample, and it's the close. You don't want the demo to end with your show fading out to silence. While you have their attention, nail down the deal. Bring back the announcer or whatever voice you used at the beginning of the demo, and forcefully tell the radio decision maker what action step you want them to take right now. Examples: "Call right now to add the show" or "Sign up today" or "Get off your butt and get on the phone" or whatever the most effective action step might be. Don't be shy. This is the time to ask for the order and get them signed up.

Killer Ingredient No. 5 - Your Contact Information

The fifth ingredient is basic, but often overlooked. Make it easy for them to contact you.

If your demo is an MP3 file, give it a file name with your show name and phone number. For example: HarryJonesShow-213-555-1212.mp3.

The MP3 file can also contain metadata: your contact info and a cover image of your show logo. (If you don't know how to add these to an MP3 file, ask any 14 year old for help. Or look up the how-to steps on a search engine.)

The worst thing you can do is name the MP3 file "DEMO". This will guarantee station executives will never be able to find it again, since their computer or phone is already filled with dozens of files from others, also titled "DEMO".

If you put your demo on a compact disc, print your contact information right on the CD. You'd be astonished how many demo discs from show hosts we've seen that are either blank or just have the word "DEMO" scribbled on them. Perhaps these folks assume that nobody else sends out demo CDs anymore. Not true, program directors still get CD demos sometimes.

Any print collateral you mail to stations is often tossed aside. But a PD might grab a CD demo to listen during their commute. If they decide to take your CD for listening in the car, why make things difficult for them? Print your contact info right on the disk itself, not just on the paper sleeve or jewel case. You score an extra point if you get the discs professionally duplicated and silkscreened.

The goal is to make saying "yes" easy, not difficult. In this day and age, when people make up their minds, they want instant results. Don't frustrate your prospects by making it difficult for them to locate you or sign up. Make it fast and easy.

Podcasters often produce an "Episode Zero" as a quick intro for new listeners, giving an overview of what to expect in later episodes. But as you have learned from this chapter, a good syndication demo is light years ahead of any Episode Zeroes you may have heard or created yourself. A really well-produced demo can truly open doors for you, and convince radio executives to put your syndicated show on the air.

Chapter Twelve

Income from Your Show

Now let's answer a question we hear most often. Just how much money can be made from a syndicated radio show? Well, this question doesn't have a simple answer. There's more than one way to make money from syndication, so let's explore the ways to profit in this field.

Probably the simplest and easiest to understand concept is direct cash payment. Let's consider that first. In this scenario, you do your show, and then you get paid cash for having done it. Simple and easy to understand, right? In this scenario, it's just like doing any job, like being a doctor, lawyer, or burger flipper at a fast-food joint. You do the job and you get paid for it. Bing, bang, boom. However, in radio syndication this scenario is rare. Unless you work for a large network or media conglomerate that owns and syndicates shows (which makes you a hired employee on the payroll), it's unlikely anyone is going to hand you cash simply for hosting a syndicated show. And if you work for a big network, then this chapter isn't going to help you much. Our financial discussion is geared toward independent syndicators, or the want-to-be syndicators hoping to convert their podcast to radio syndication.

So what if you are an independent syndicator? Why won't someone pay you cash for your show? You might be saying, "Hey, it's a great show. It's very entertaining and informative. I have a great personality. I'll bring lots of listeners to radio stations that run my syndicated show. That alone must be worth money. So why won't they me pay cash for it?"

Well, unless you're a syndication superstar, it's unlikely that any radio station will pay you cash for the honor of broadcasting your show. This is because stations get most syndicated shows for free. That's right. Radio stations receive most syndicated programming for zippo. They simply sign up for the shows they want and those programs come rolling in the door with no cash outlay required. All the radio station has to do is agree to broadcast the show in its entirety, including the commercials. Ah-ha, commercials! Now we're getting someplace.

Barter Commercials

It's the ads that will make the real money for you. In fact, ads are what make most of the money in the entire commercial radio industry. In syndication, stations receive shows in exchange for the station giving ad minutes to the syndicator. This exchange of commercial minutes for programming is called barter (or trade). You probably know what barter means. It's an honored way of doing business that goes back to the beginning of humankind, where someone bartered (or traded) something of value for something else.

For example, Mr. Farmer barters corn with Mr. Blacksmith, and in exchange, Mr. Blacksmith puts new horseshoes on Mr. Farmer's horses. No cash changed hands, only objects of value. Get the idea?

In radio syndication, you provide the valuable program, and the radio station barters commercial minutes for it. Once you own those valuable commercial minutes, that's what you use to make money.

Some people find this a little confusing because they're not used to doing business this way. But think about the farmer and the blacksmith example we just used. The farmer barters his corn to the blacksmith who takes the corn and then puts new shoes on the farmer's horses. Now the blacksmith has 25 bushels of corn. He certainly can't eat all that corn, so what does he do with it? He sells it for cash to hungry people and earns himself some cash. Now, the blacksmith has big bucks and everybody's happy.

Still confused? Maybe this will clarify your thinking.

If you own your own successful syndicated radio show, that means you will end up owning some commercial minutes that run on lots of radio stations.

"So what?" you may say. Well, those minutes can be very valuable. How valuable?

Let's look at TV for an easy example. Everyone's heard of Oprah Winfrey, who for many years hosted a daily, syndicated TV show. She owned her show and likewise owned a few minutes of commercial time within the syndicated show. Those few ad minutes helped make her one of the richest women in entertainment, worldwide. But what about radio?

Without naming names, one superstar of radio syndication earns about $20 million a year. And a famous radio syndication host sold her show for over ten million.

This value mostly derives from the commercials that run in those shows. So you can see that the ad minutes in barter syndication can be worth a bundle.

But what about a start-up show, new to syndication? Let's explore income possibilities at that level.

105

Minimum National Audience

A successful syndicated radio show must reach a minimum national audience. If you're just starting, you need to keep doing the show until it grows to fruition, while maintaining the quality of the show. If you do those things, and keep adding stations, you can build a steady national ad revenue stream. There are billions of dollars in this industry, so even a relatively small share can be worth a significant sum. Believe that it's there for you, if you do things right and your show captures an audience.

Value Depends on Audience Size

As we said, the key to success in syndication is reaching a minimum national audience. If your show is properly produced and marketed, and it reaches that minimum threshold of listeners, then your show will support national radio advertising and you will see those ad revenues flowing to you. In the marketplace for national syndicated radio advertising, much of the big ad money is allocated using a formula called Cost Per Point (CPP). A full explanation of CPP goes beyond the scope of this book, but just be aware that national ad buyers use this formula to calculate and compare ad media costs.

National Sales Representation

If your syndicated radio show is already heard on a significant number of stations, and it has a sufficiently large total audience, then radio networks and syndicators will be happy to sell the ads in your show on a commission basis.

For this to happen, your show's total national audience will ideally be one-tenth of a national rating point (0.1 rating), or greater. Anything smaller than that audience usually won't interest the national ad sellers. There is only so much time in the day, and these pros would much rather spend their precious time selling ads in bigger shows that pay higher rates, rather than handling start-up shows with low potential returns.

There are some networks and syndicators that will consolidate the audiences of smaller shows, into one larger and sellable network for advertisers. Of course, the money you will earn in such a situation will be divided among all the participants, but this is a way to get some cash from your show if it's only on a few stations so far. You really want to grow your audience and station list to the point where your show can be sold on its own, for maximum profits and income.

We are sometimes asked, "How many stations do I need to sign up, for my show to reach one-tenth of a rating point?" There is no single answer to this question. Here's why.

Various stations have different audience sizes. If your show is picked up by the biggest stations in top markets, you may only need a handful of stations to qualify for national sales representation. But if your show is carried by small and medium size stations, you may need several dozen stations to qualify. Most shows will be picked up by a variety of stations with different audience sizes, so you can see there is no single answer to the "how many stations do I need" question.

Here's the bottom line: a newly syndicated show probably won't attract the interest of big networks or ad-selling reps, simply because the total audience isn't yet big enough for them to sell to big advertisers.

So how can your show generate income in the meantime?

We are going to share a unique strategy to help you do just that. And as we've mentioned, there is a process involved. Don't worry, you won't need sales training and there's no need to be pushy or "salesy" to make this happen. The next chapter will explain how.

Chapter Thirteen

System for Ad Sales

We're going to share one way to generate revenue and profits from your syndicated radio show, even in its earliest days. This strategy can also be applied to selling ads in your podcast.

Selling Ads is a Multistep Process

As we've said, there's a certain amount of prep work needed before you'll be ready to sell ads in your show. The preliminary steps are all pretty easy.

In our opinion, it's much better for you to take care of these important prep steps first, rather than risk blowing it with a potential advertiser by trying to pitch them before you have your act together.

A syndicated radio show can deliver consistent revenue just like clockwork. That's a tremendous advantage of syndication over other forms of media and over many other career paths you could take.

This financial scenario may sound too good to be true, but it is no pie in the sky, get rich quick scheme. It's a reality for people we've coached and for others who followed the steps to become successful syndicated radio hosts. It can happen for you too.

Nothing Comes From Nothing

Understand that there will be an investment phase at the beginning of the syndication process. You must put in some time and effort, and spend some dollars to create and build your show. Nothing comes from nothing. Just like a farmer, you have to plant the seeds, tend them, water them and allow time until it grows to harvest.

For some people, the idea of investing any funds to launch a syndicated radio show seems like a financial stretch. Given the potential long term rewards, we don't think it's all that much. But if your current situation means you don't have two dimes to rub together, there is good news. In an upcoming chapter, we'll explain how to connect with investors who can fund the launch and growth of your show.

Common Misperceptions

We're about to destroy a few common misperceptions about how to go about selling ads in a well-niched, syndicated radio show. These may well be the most important things you'll learn about how to sell ads. Then we'll get to the key steps involved in our revenue creating process.

What do you think is the most common approach taken by new show hosts and novice ad sales people who try to sell ads in a syndicated radio show? Well, let's examine the typical approach the rookies take.

Friends and Family

First, if it's something they've been thinking about, a beginner may start by asking friends, family, and associates if they know anyone who might buy some ads. It's human nature. When there is uncertainty, we typically ask the people around us for help. We might even turn to a business owner we know, to ask if there's a product or service they want to promote.

If the rookie seller doesn't get immediate rejection, then something worse can happen. They may get pummeled with questions they're unable to confidently answer. Questions such as, what are your rates for 30s versus 60s? How many people will hear my ads and who exactly are they? What other advertisers run in the show? What's the qualitative and quantitative profile of your listeners? Do you have a media kit you can show me? Can I try running free ads and pay you if they work?

The questions can be confusing. If a potential advertiser has some media savvy, they might throw in some lingo: How many gross impressions will I get? What's the CPM or cost per thousand? Or, if it's a web-based prospect, the questions might be: How many unique visitors? What's the sticky factor? What's the click-through rate?

A novice show host may feel intimidated and confused by these questions. They may promise to find the answers (once they learn the answers), but a clear impression has been made. You're a newbie and you don't know much about selling ads.

Trying to sell ads in your show without proper preparation is not the way to have success. However, you get extra points because you're learning the right way to do things to avoid potential mistakes.

Prepare Before You Pitch

If you want to start selling ads in your show, forget about figuring out your ad rates, forget about creating a media kit, and forget about putting together a sales presentation. And do not make contact with potential ad buyers. Don't do any of that for now.

111

The very first thing you must do is determine the right market for your show ads.

Ask yourself this question: "Who in the world might possibly get really excited about buying commercials in my radio show?"

Do some thinking. Decide what category of advertisers might want to buy radio ads in your show. Which businesses would be the ideal, perfect matches for your show? Who would love to reach the people who are in your listening audience? Answer these questions to the best of your ability, before doing anything else.

This is all about focusing in on the niche of your particular show, something we already covered. Determine who the players are in your niche. Who would most benefit from being exposed to your listeners, and vice versa? This is the task that goes first, at the very beginning of the ad sales process. Seek out the answer to this key question. Everything else will follow from the results of this research.

Here's an example. Let's say you do a late night radio talk show that discusses UFOs, alien invasions, and other creepy topics, including the possible end of the world. Now this might sound like a very tough sell with most advertisers, but think carefully about who would want to reach the late night listeners who love these topics. We can think of a few potential ad buyers.

How about companies catering to survivalists -- those who think the end IS near, and want to plan ahead? These might include sponsors that sell freeze-dried food, emergency power supplies, fallout shelters, insurance policies, radiation detectors, camping gear, rechargeable flashlights and radios, and even gold bullion. These would all be plausible prospects.

If this example sounds a little farfetched, we're actually talking about a real life show, which has these very advertisers. Perhaps you can guess the name, it's a syndicated show that delves into weird topics. Their advertisers fit the categories we just mentioned. Since these ads are heard again and again, they must be reaching responsive listeners who are ideal customers for their products.

Dig Deep In Your Niche

Let's take another example, one we mentioned earlier, *The Home Office Hour*. What products or services are specific to people who have a home office? Don't just think of the most obvious answers. Yes, these people need furniture, a computer and office supplies. But if that's all you came up with, you're missing the point. Really hone in on the special things that ONLY home office users (listeners to that show) might buy.

How about a cool product that mutes the doorbell, so it won't ding-dong while the owner's in a middle of a big telephone sales pitch? Or an affordable office phone system that has extensions, puts callers on hold and plays music to them, just like at a big office?

Most home office owners want to come across to others as bigger than they really are. Any product that helps them do this is ideal for *Home Office Hour* listeners. If that niched advertiser gets results, they might just invest their entire ad budget with the show.

But you don't have to only target small companies that make oddball products. If a major advertiser is eager to reach your targeted audience because of a niche product they're marketing, there's a chance you can land that big fish. So the first step is to focus on your show's niche and research who might invest ad dollars to reach that niche.

Researching Potential Advertisers

You might wonder how to do this research. The answer varies. But if you are knowledgeable about the topic of your show, you may already know of some category leaders in your niche and how they market themselves.

Let's say your show is about vegetarian food. Stroll through a specialty food store catering to this group and you'll see the names of leading companies that market products just for vegetarians.

Once you've developed a list of names of these business prospects, your research doesn't stop there. Next, find out how these companies currently market themselves. Explore the web. Look through specialty publications. This will give you lots of important info.

Researching Your Audience

Along with studying your potential advertisers, study your listening audience. What products and services do you think they're interested in? Of course you can do this on a limited basis by dialoguing with listeners one-to-one. We are not suggesting you do this on the air during your show, but off the air, with listeners you come in contact with.

Still, one-to-one dialogue with fans isn't really going to get you much actionable information. Here is a more meaningful way to research and study your listeners. Use one of the online survey website firms. For example, as of this writing, the web site SurveyMonkey.com will let you conduct a free 10-question survey with a maximum of 100 responses. And if you spend just a few bucks, they will let you conduct a survey with a thousand responses. (We have no connection to this web site.)

Online Listener Survey

It's easy to create an online survey online, and then ask your listeners to participate. Promote the survey during your show and encourage participation with a prize drawing of some goodie your listeners would find attractive.

We do not suggest saying it's a survey for advertisers, as that might scare people off. Just give the perfectly honest explanation that you wish to learn more about your listeners, and you have a nice reward if they'll participate. There's no need for them to give their names or any information other than an email to participate (you will need emails to send out prize rewards).

In creating your survey, you might ask listeners to share how much they typically spend on certain products or services, how often they buy them, and so on. For example, if you do a show about cars, you might ask, how much do you typically spend on automotive accessories in a year? Where do you buy these products online, which sites do you prefer? Specific info like this can be pure gold for advertisers.

The beauty of these online survey sites is they can give you neatly tabulated results at the click of a button. You end up with a survey that is presentable to potential advertisers who will likely be impressed -- especially if they can clearly see the close fit between their marketing message and your targeted audience. If there's a very good match, it will make logical sense for them to try running ads in your show.

Top Rates with a Small Audience

Now, here's the beauty of this entire approach to advertising. If you can convince an advertiser that your built-in audience is perfectly targeted to their needs, you can command good rates despite having a relatively small audience.

You may be reading this and wondering if this approach is grounded in reality. Do people actually make money following the steps I've just outlined? Yes, they certainly do and some of them make a surprising amount of money. This is also true for the podcasts that follow this approach to ad sales.

Two examples of moneymaking shows have been written up in the mainstream media. The first is a wine radio show that has a total audience of only 15,000 listeners, yet, the hosts have sold 60-second ads in their show for over $1,000 each.

Targeted Audiences Get Advertisers Excited

Why would advertisers eagerly spend over a grand to buy a single ad, to only reach a total audience of 15,000? For one reason – this show delivers an audience consisting only of fanatic wine lovers. Many of these listeners probably buy wine online. For some wine drinkers, money is no object. Since virtually everyone listening to the show is into fine wine, the smart advertiser gets a big bang for the buck, with very little waste.

A wine company might spend far more elsewhere for ads reaching a general audience. But there will also be lots of waste, because not everyone in a general audience drinks wine. In fact, many do not. But, in the case of this show, the ads are targeted so there's virtually zero waste. Advertisers reach an enthusiastic wine-loving audience. This is why they'll pay above the normal rate for the ads.

No surprise, the show hosts have a media kit which contains the charts and graphs they got from doing surveys of their listening audience.

Here's another example. It's a radio show about being a better mom. Topics include raising healthy and happy kids, juggling career and motherhood, and other angles on being a modern mom. The hosts are moms too, not professional ad sellers.

Yet these hosts sold an ad package priced over $100,000.00 to a disposable paper goods company. And they renewed this deal three years in a row. Why would an advertiser spend that much to reach a relatively small audience? Because they know that moms with small kids really love disposable paper goods!

The research shows that the audience contains only moms, listening for how to be better at raising kids. It's a laser-focused target.

Audience Before Income

You may be scratching your head right about now. If your show isn't on the air yet, and you were hoping to sign up some advertisers to pay the bills before you have an audience established, that will be difficult.

Unless you are a known celebrity or you have strong social media appeal, or your show has a recognized brand name behind it, the reality is this: it will be difficult to sell ads before your show gets on stations.

You must first launch the show, attract at least a minimal number of listeners, and then go after the advertisers.

If you're someone who really needs cash to fund the launch of your show, then read our upcoming suggestions on how to secure investors to back the startup of your program.

Relationships Rule

Just about every rule has an exception, and that is the case here. Here is the one exception to everything we just said. If you have a business connection or personal relationship with someone who might want to run some ads, and that person already knows and trusts you, then it may be possible to get that first time advertiser to buy into your unproven show. Even if that special somebody buys your ads early in the game, don't expect them to be an endless pipeline of funds unless you can eventually deliver results for them.

Chapter Fourteen

Ad Sales Strategy Review

Let's summarize the sales steps we've covered so far. These are the steps you should take before you try selling any ads in your show.

Step No. 1 - Determine Your Target Market

First, you must determine the specific target market of advertisers you wish to secure. For example, if your radio show is all about creating the perfect backyard garden, you need to build a list of potential ad buyers wanting to reach people who love gardening. These might include sellers of weed remover gadgets, or plant nutrients, or automatic watering devices, and so on. Any of these would be ideal advertisers for a gardening show.

Let's say your show is about golf. There are golf resort destinations that might want to run ads, especially if you agree to host the show live from their resort. And there are companies that sell golf accessories, gift items for golfers, and so on. These could all be good targets for your ad pitch, especially if your listener survey indicates they like to buy these products.

Step No. 2 - Research the Potential Advertisers

Second, you should learn how particular advertisers currently market their goods and services. What media do they use, such as specialty magazines or search engine ads? You can often get an idea of their advertising budget, based on how often their ads appear and the type of media they use to advertise. Go to a major online search engine, put in some common search key words related to these companies, and see what ads appear.

Facebook is another platform that will display ads relating to your interests. In this case, if you join some golf-related Facebook groups, you will probably be served ads for golf products and services.

The more different ads that appear in a category, the greater is the competition among these businesses. In those cases, they are likely to pay more per click. A major campaign on a search engine or on social media can the advertiser a bundle. How often do you see their ads? This can give you a rough idea of their ad budgets.

Speaking of search engines, you can sometimes learn a lot about your prospective advertisers by simply roaming the web and gathering information. Do some online research and you may find advertisers relating to the topic of your show.

You might also do some social engineering to determine how and where a prospective advertiser markets themselves. By social engineering, we mean making connections with those who may be willing to share some inside info with you.

It could be someone you meet at an industry event or a business networking session, or someone you connect with at an online message board.

You might find a knowledgeable person any place where insiders in your niche tend to congregate. Sometimes, the right person will happily open up and spill all the beans. Or, they'll refer you to someone who has the answers you seek.

Step No. 3 - Learn More about Your Audience

At the same time you're researching possible advertisers and building a list of potential sponsors who might want to run ads in your show, you'll want to learn a lot more about your audience. As we mentioned, conduct an online survey using one of the web survey sites (such as surveymonkey.com) and learn about your listeners' shopping preferences, buying decisions, wish lists, and goals.

If you host that golf show we mentioned a few pages ago, you might ask these survey questions of your audience: How much do you spend on golf equipment? How many golf vacations do you take a year? Where are your favorite destinations? How much do you spend on dining in a year? How do you decide where to go? Which websites do you use to research golf vacations? What are your favorite golf-related websites? And so on.

While you're at it, ask them to share some demographic information such as their age, sex, single or married. Do they have kids? What's their approximate income level, and so on. This info will be very helpful when you aggregate the survey results. It will let your potential advertisers see the makeup of your listening audience and help them see how it fits their advertising needs.

Be True to Your Niche

As you've realized by now, it would be a mistake to make your show about all things to all people. Be true to your niche and it will be true to you. In other words, if you want to make money doing your syndicated show, then don't attempt to do a radio show that covers every topic under the sun.

Successful syndicated shows need a specific topic, otherwise known as a "hook", some niche that attracts a set of listeners and a set of advertisers as well.

It is a wasted effort trying to secure big general advertisers at the beginning when your show's just getting its legs. Instead, take a pinpoint approach, like throwing a well-aimed dart to hit the bull's eye. Focus on specific advertisers that may best fit your listening audience's needs and interests. Then watch your income rise.

" HAROLD, WE NEED TO TALK. "

What Separates You From the Pack?

What does your show contain, that no other show contains? What sets it apart and makes it unique? And what about the makeup of your listening audience that makes your show valuable to advertisers? This last question is what really drives your revenue as it did in the examples we mentioned a little while ago.

One thing we haven't specifically mentioned yet is audience size.

When you're selling ads in a niched show, audience numbers are far less important and that's a good thing for you, if you have a small audience.

Determining Audience Size

Some potential ad buyers will insist upon knowing the approximate size of your audience. How many are listening, they will ask?

One very rough way to determine this for your syndicated show is to ask each station on your network to provide its listenership numbers. Then add them up to find your total audience. Again, this will be an inexact, rough approximation.

A more precise approach is to ask a research company, reputable network or syndication company to determine your total audience based on actual ratings information.

Now you've spent some time gathering the info you need. You've looked around and spotted some likely advertisers for your show, and put together a list of them. Hopefully, you have a fair understanding of the makeup of your show's audience, buying habits, and interests. You've compiled that or better yet, you had an online survey company neatly compile it for you. Maybe you have some national research data to show the strength of your audience versus the general population. You may also have data on how many listeners you have.

Next Steps in the Process

Good news! Most of the hard work is done. You're nearly ready to start contacting potential advertisers about buying ads in your show.

A radio show consists of sound waves. There are no moving pictures or printed pages, when it comes to radio. To really convince advertisers to hand over their money, you'll need more than just sound waves. They will want a physical embodiment of what your show is all about, something to hand them, mail them, or email them. Something they can read later and show to others.

In a previous chapter, we discussed the PDF sell sheet which you send to program directors at radio stations.

With some slight modifications, you can use this same PDF to pitch advertisers as well. It's good to have if you're serious about selling ads.

The PDF sell sheet we mentioned in a previous chapter is meant to convince radio stations to carry your show. The PDF for advertisers is meant to convince advertisers to buy ads in your show. And if you have some survey results, you can add those as separate pages and create an simple but impressive sales kit to give to potential advertisers.

An Effective Media Kit

Here's what we suggest you include in a sell sheet for potential advertisers.

Initial impressions are important, and a nice looking PDF says a lot of good things about your show. First, start with your show logo at the top.

Next, have a photo of you the host, followed by a bullet-point summary of your show. At the bottom, include your contact information.

This PDF is a main, general information page, but please don't pack it full of text. Leave some open space and make the page an easy read with some nice graphics. Resist the urge to pack the page full of words. As graphic designers like to say, "Let it breathe." You can do a second page with a bio of the host and a third page with listener testimonials and people's comments about how great your show is.

The Rate Card

You can also create a "rate card" to show your ad pricing details. This usually isn't an actual card, but a regular size page listing the advertiser options in a menu or grid style. It will show the standard rates you charge for each option.

Instead of a general rate card, you may wish to do a customized rate sheet for each advertiser you approach. That is much more personal, and it allows you to adjust your rates based on the advertiser's potential budget, and special ad options you're offering to each prospect. By the way, if you're wondering how to figure the pricing of the ads in your show, don't worry because we're going to cover that topic very shortly.

Other Ingredients

Let's go back to the media kit, and its contents. You should include a summary of your listeners' survey information (and any other research you have) on one or two easy to read, well laid out pages. This will mean a lot to any smart advertiser, as their entire buying decision may well hinge on what the research says.

One more item you can include is a simple cover note that sums up everything for the prospect and reminds them you'll follow up shortly.

Another way to provide all this information is to have your web site display the pages. Some prospects may want to print it out, so we suggest making the entire media kit downloadable in PDF form.

By the way, if you want to see a sample media kit like the one we just described, along with a sample radio advertising agreement, and so on, that is all available as a free download for readers of this book. Just navigate to http://www.FreeRadioInfo.com and get an instant free download of these business essentials and much more. See page 163 of this book for details on the free Podcast To Broadcast "Power Tools" and claim your free download.

The Advertising Agreement

Speaking of the contract, what must be included in it? Actually, any business agreement can be boiled down to the following key points: the names of the two parties, the goods or services provided, the timeframe, and the compensation. In the case of your radio advertising agreement, you'll want to include the start and end dates of the advertising schedule when the ads will be heard on your show, the length of the ads, and the price of the ads. There are many more things you can put into an agreement, those are the basics. Even just a simple letter that lays out the terms of the deal will be okay, as long as both parties can sign at the bottom. (Keep in mind, we are not legal experts or attorneys. For competent legal advice, please seek a professional.)

Now you should have a list of potential advertisers, some info about your listeners, and your media kit. You're ready to start selling! Of course, you can add more weaponry to your sales arsenal as time goes by.

Pricing Your Commercials

Let's turn to three ways you can price your commercial inventory. How you price the ads in your show will of course, determine the money you will make.

If you've ever purchased a plane ticket, you've no doubt experienced what the airlines call "yield management." This is a variable pricing strategy that affects airfares. It is driven by three factors: competition, demand, and inventory.

The next time you fly, try this. Introduce yourself to the passenger sitting next to you and after you've chatted for a few minutes, ask them what they'd mind telling you what they paid for their seat. Chances are it will different from what you paid, sometimes shockingly different.

The reason that airlines use this complex pricing system is simple. If they don't sell all the seats before takeoff, those potential earnings are gone forever once the plane leaves the gate. There's no way to recoup revenue for unsold seats on a jet plane. Yet, they don't want to price all the seats too low or they won't make enough money. In a nutshell, that's the reason for their "yield management" system.

Yield Management Explained

Much the same holds true for the ad inventory in your syndicated show. Once the show is produced and broadcast, it's generally not possible to add spots to the unsold positions. So, the unsold inventory in your show becomes worthless at the moment the show is broadcast. It's just like when the plane takes off with empty seats. One exception for radio is the Internet, where on-demand shows can have spots inserted later in the process. However, not many advertisers want to run their spots in old shows, unless your show is a hot niche property.

Let's return to the concept of yield management. How do the airlines deal with this? They use extremely complex computer software to manage their seat inventory and pricing for maximum yield. They also factor in considerable amounts of behavioral research and behavioral modeling to make careful predictions about each flight's seating inventory, based on the day of the week and time of year. We're not going to get that sophisticated, but we can take a page from their book to maximize your radio show ad sales revenue.

Multiple Price Categories

Consider breaking down your ad sales into three price categories. You can of course add more categories later if you wish.

The first pricing level might be for your long-term, high volume advertisers, willing to make a long-term commitment to advertise on your show for 52 weeks, or perhaps 39 weeks or 26 weeks at a time.

Category No. 1 - Long Term Advertisers

Let us say a long-term advertiser agrees to buy a spot or two every week for 52 weeks. Just like a gold status or premium level airline passenger who buys lots of tickets, this top advertiser deserves a nice discount and some perks too. It's similar to your decision to buy the giant, jumbo package of paper towels at the bulk warehouse store, you pay a lower price because you're buying so much at one time.

You can create a pricing grid, with the lowest unit ad price for a 52 week buy. Then the next (higher) price level would be 39 weeks, and then 26 weeks. In each case, the longer the commitment, the better the price break. And maybe you throw in some bonus ads for the big spenders, too. With this scenario, the 52 week advertiser pays less per spot. The good news is you get long-term income, which saves you time and effort. Since those spots are sold for a full year, the work of selling that inventory is done.

Category No. 2 - Short Term Advertisers

Now consider a second pricing level. This one might be for shorter term ad buys. These are the sponsors who have some time-specific needs, such as a two week sale or promotion. Or perhaps they want to give your show a short-term test to see how it works for them. What do the airlines do when a random ticket buyer shows up and needs one seat, for a specific day and time? They make those passengers ante up and pay a high rate.

In your case, somebody buying a few spots would pay a higher rate. (Make sure these advertisers are aware that longer commitment gets a price break and bonuses. They just might go for it.)

Category No. 3 - Last-Minute Advertisers

How about a third pricing level for your show? It's getting close to broadcast time and you have some unsold slots to fill. In that case, anything above a minimum price may be better than nothing. You won't get a penny if those slots go unsold.

How do the airlines industry handle this situation?

You've probably guessed the answer. Stand-by fliers are those who pay a super low price, with no guarantee of when they'll fly, which seat they'll get, or even if they'll fly at all. You can do the same with unsold radio show inventory and never do a show with unsold spots again. In radio, ads to fill unsold slots are sometimes called "remainder inventory," because they're what remains after all the other spots are sold.

Remainder Ad Sales

Rather than put any effort into week to week selling of remainder inventory, you can make advance arrangements with certain businesses or individuals willing to pay a very low ad rate in exchange for being totally flexible about when their ads will air. You could even trade or barter them for products or services, such as restaurant meals.

You would want to pitch this to smaller and sideline businesses that don't have the budget for a solid ad schedule.

There are also companies that make a business of selling remainder radio ad inventory on a daily basis. Look them up online to learn more. There might be an opportunity for you there.

Category No. 4 - Packaged Advertising Buyers

While we're talking about ways to price your ads, let's throw in a fourth pricing approach. That is to package the radio ads together with other advertising and promotions you offer. These extras might include contests, online ads, web banners, clickable logos, links, product endorsements, live appearances, and so on.

Promotions such as these can 'plus up' your ad rates to substantially higher levels. This is mainly because the advertiser feels they're getting much greater value by receiving a package of goods, as opposed to just some radio ads.

You can now see there are different ways to price and sell your ad inventory. Of course, the goal is always to maximize your total revenue.

Take time to explore this topic further on your own. Our brief explanation is meant to highlight this point, and make you aware of different ways to price your spots beyond the traditional rate card or standard pricing approach.

Eventually, there should be less need for you to experiment with rates and packaging. Once you discover some effective price points that work well (and that make your advertisers happy), stick with that winning formula and watch your revenue grow.

Premium Niche Pricing

We've explained in some detail how to calculate the approximate value of your show's ad inventory. If you happen to host a specialized and focused show with a very marketable audience of reasonable size, the rules go out the window. You can realistically push your rates higher by 25 percent, 50 percent, 100 percent or even more. In these cases, the basic pricing rules do not apply.

Now it is a matter of what the market will bear and frankly, how gutsy you want to be in pitching your show to bigger advertisers. Big advertisers have big budgets and they are used to spending lots of money on marketing. So a high rate won't bother them as long as they see the value in reaching your premium listeners.

Ask for the Order

Asking for what may seem to you like an incredibly high rate and actually getting it, can come down to something as simple as keeping your cool during a meeting or phone call.

We will share a quick story here. We saw this happen at a radio station in a major market. One day, the station hired a new salesperson. The fellow didn't seem to have much on the ball. But one day this fellow returned from a sales call and handed in an order with the highest spot rate that the station had ever received. The manager's eyes were wide in astonishment.

When asked how he got such a sky-high rate, the salesman replied that he was asked by a potential new client for a quick price quote on ads. At that moment, the sales guy couldn't recall the actual rates, his mind went blank. So he just threw out a huge round number that popped into his head at the moment, in a confident tone of voice. To his surprise and delight, the prospect instantly agreed and the deal was done.

It wasn't until the salesman returned to the station that he learned how many times over the normal rate he'd actually gotten.

We are not suggesting that you sell ads in your show by making up rates. But that story is a good illustration of the power of being direct in a sales transaction. If the prospect and you seem to be on the same wavelength, and you're confident your show would be an ideal fit for them, don't hesitate to quote a serious rate. The worst that could happen is they say, "No." But even then, you'll have plenty of room to negotiate.

And if you have some research to back up the value of your show, don't be shy about asking a high spot rate, as long as you can carry it off with confidence.

Rejection is Part of the Game

We stated this in an earlier chapter but it's worth mentioning again. You must understand that in both signing up stations and selling ads, rejection is just part of the game. There will always be people who say "no" when you approach them about buying ads, no matter how well prepared you are or how wonderful your show may be.

Don't dwell on the turndowns. Just keep moving forward. The mission in sales is to get past all the No's and find the next Yes that is out there. Don't take the turn downs personally.

Follow Up Fast

Another "do" is to follow up quickly with anyone who expresses even the slightest interest in your show. Timing is critical. Once a potential buyer cools off it may be very hard to warm them back up again.

Strike while the iron is hot, and while that prospect is actively considering the idea of buying into your show.

Know Your 'Story' Inside and Out

Another "do" is to file away in your brain the advantages of advertising in your show. Some marketers like to call this the "story." You need to know the story about your product. Practice telling it over and over again, until you get it down pat.

This is because a question you will likely hear will be, why should I run spots in your show?

If you have your story down pat, you'll have plenty of convincing reasons to share, without missing a beat.

Put all the bullet points about your show on paper, but more importantly, have these benefits memorized and in your brain. When someone asks you why they should consider your show, it's impressive if you have a compelling story to tell, including a few commanding reasons to buy your show. But if you stammer and stumble, and try to make up an answer right there on the spot, you obviously won't be convincing and you may lose a potential customer.

Don't Make These Mistakes

Now, let's touch on some of the "don'ts" of syndication spot sales.

As we said before, don't ask people to advertise in your show until you have your act together. You need to finalize your advertising details, your rates and so on.

It is human nature to immediately start asking those people you know if they'd ever consider running ads in your show. But don't say a word about selling ads until you're ready and able to follow through with them. Otherwise, you'll risk losing some of your choicest prospects when they realize you're just talking through your hat, and you don't have any important details pinned down yet.

Treat this as a highly professional transaction, even with those you count as friends or business associates, and they'll take you seriously. After all, you're talking about having these folks hand over money to you. So, you want to come across as a solid pro.

Another 'don't' -- don't worry that you aren't a born salesperson! A common statement we hear from syndicators who want to get spots sold in their show is, "I'm no good at sales. I don't like rejection." To this we say, "Who does?" Is there a human being on earth who likes hearing the word "no"? But, many people who successfully sell ads have learned to keep things in perspective.

To repeat this important point: a "no" to an ad buy is NOT a rejection of you. It's just part of doing business. If somebody isn't interested in your offer, you move to the next prospect and see if they're interested. In doing so, you'll probably discover new ways to refine your offer based on the turndowns, and make an even stronger offer to the next prospect.

When Ads Are Sold, Follow Up

Here's a third 'don't' when it comes to sales. Don't assume the work is done the moment someone buys an ad. Once an ad campaign is sold, you want to make sure things happen just as you promised, so the customer ends up happy.

That will encourage them to become a repeat customer. And that will make your job easier and more profitable. Each repeat customer is someone you don't have to sell to again. They're already sold on you and your show. Ask your happiest customers to give you testimonials, which will become powerful sales tools for you.

One of the most common complaints in the world of business is that companies jump through every hoop and promise the moon when they want somebody to buy something. It's as if you can't get them to leave you alone.

But once the customer buys (so the complaint goes), the company seems to disappear. Many of the services that were promised are faulty, limited, or nonexistent.

Good Service Will Build Your Business

But the business people who follow through with good service and attention after the sale are those who reap the long term rewards, because quality service has become a rarity today. When an advertising client has a really great experience with your show, they will tell others about it. They may even send new clients to your door.

It doesn't take a whole lot for you to be considered among the best. All it takes are a few extra touches, such as a personal thank you note when they sign up, for example. Friendly touches like these are never forgotten and go a long way in the harried world of commerce.

Of course, you must also be sure that all your business practices are on track, so the client's order runs smoothly, at the right time, and with the right copy.

If you do all the basics, and then do a little more than expected (perhaps throw in some free bonus spots when you have unsold time), you will help to establish a long term relationship.

Closing the Deal, In Depth

Speaking of service and follow through, let's delve a little further into the topic of closing the deal. Your goal is to get their signature on the agreement. This is a point where deals can unexpectedly fall apart. Everything seems to be going well, the prospect appears to be in sync with you, but when it comes to actually doing the deal, it just doesn't get done.

The tried and true advice of the long time sales veterans is helpful here. First, understand that there's no magic to closing a deal. It should just flow naturally out of the rest of your presentation.

Ideally, you should be asking some very leading questions through the entire conversation. You should be talking about the proposed deal with the firm assumption that the prospect will sign up. If you notice that things seem to be stalling between you and the prospect in the last moments before they commit to the deal, the following suggestions may be helpful to you.

Words Are Important

First, erase the word "if" from your vocabulary. Never say to a prospect "if you sign up" or use similar tentative phrases. Instead, go for it. Be definitive! For example, you could say "You're going to be really happy when you sign this agreement, because here's what will happen".

Or you might say, "As our valued client, here's what you're going to receive". Another statement you might make could be, "Your commercials in our show will not only sound great, they will make great things happen for your business." In short, don't pussyfoot around in your wording. Sound positive, enthusiastic and certain about results.

When it's time to ask for their signature on the contract, don't waltz around. You can ask them a classic closing question, one that has a "yes, yes" answer. For example, "Which plan would you prefer, the 52 week plan or the 39 week plan?"

A question like this assumes they will do business with you, because the only way to answer that question is for them to agree to the deal.

This may sound a little corny, but it does works. It's much like the car dealer who says, "Do you want your new car to be blue or red?"

No matter how you answer, you're buying a car. The same holds true with buying spots in your show.

Seal the Deal

What's also very important is what happens after you get the signature. This is commonly called "sealing the deal". It is best to do this soon after the deal is signed, to avoid any chances of buyer's remorse. It can be as simple as sending them a strong, well-written letter telling them what a great decision they just made. Or, you could send the new client a thank you note, gift basket or other nice item to welcome them. While none of this is required, you'll find it will be good for your business. Sealing the deal will cement the relationship you worked so hard to forge with your new advertising client.

Quick Income Ideas

Let's move on now with the answer to another common sales question. What are some ways to get quick income in syndication when you don't have the time to apply the entire ad selling process? Well, one approach is to find a company that handles "per inquiry" or PI radio ads. These are professional sounding ads that you run in your show in unsold slots.

Most PI's contain a toll free number or text so listeners can respond if they want more info. Or they might use another direct response mechanism, such as a specific web address. You get paid based on how many of your listeners called or texted or visited the website, or ordered the product. Don't expect to get rich on these PI ads, but they can provide a modest income. To find such a company, search the web for "per inquiry radio ads." But choose carefully, as some of these companies are more reliable than others.

Another variation on this idea is to find a reputable online seller (ideally, a small company or an individual) that could use more traffic at their website. You promote their web site in ads on your show. The site owner then pays you, based on the number of leads you deliver to their site.

Affiliate Programs

An alternative to this idea is to build a simple website yourself and fill it with commission generating web ads. These are often referred to online as "affiliate programs." Some companies that provide these type of web ads include Commission Junction (CJ.com), Amazon.com, JVZoo.com, and ClickBank.com.

You promote your commission generating website during your show as an online source of special deals for your listeners. Whenever a visitor clicks on the ads or buys a product or service, you get a commission. Some of the commissions can be substantial, and this is a way to generate income for you. Of course, if you have any products or services you wish to sell, you can create radio ads for yourself and promote your own offerings to your audience.

Selling Your Own Products

Let's discuss products sales for a moment, because this can be a meaningful way to derive income from your show. There are many items you can create and offer, such as information products such as e-books, video trainings, audio seminars, and more. These can focus on your area of expertise, and you can offer these to your listeners at an e-commerce website. As a syndicated host, you're viewed as an expert and authority in your niche. This automatically lends you the credibility that helps to sell such products.

Promo items such as hats, t-shirts, and bags can also be sold, especially if your show has a cool looking logo (one that your listeners will be proud to display). Companies such as CafePress.com make it a snap to sell goods like these.

If you have seriously loyal listeners, you might even consider requesting donations from listeners to support your show. Before you dismiss this idea, keep in mind that contributions are a vital source of income for public radio stations. If this approach works for them, it just might work for you.

Chapter Fifteen

Funding From Outsiders

Let's turn to a topic that may be of interest to you if you need financial help to launch your syndicated radio show. It doesn't cost a fortune to start a show in syndication. But for some, even a relatively small amount of funds may be out of reach.

Before we explain how to find investors to fund your syndicated radio show project, recall a common error we mentioned in a previous chapter. That mistake is trying to sell ads in your show before you are fully prepared. That rule is even more applicable when it comes to finding investors for your show.

Do Your Homework First

If you start asking investors for financial backing, and they get a sense you really don't know exactly how much you need or even what you're talking about, you'll get shot down faster than you can believe. Try going back later when you have things more organized, and you'll usually find their skepticism is high due to the poor initial impression you made. The same holds true if you hope to obtain a bank loan.

You must do a little homework first. You've got to prepare ahead of time before you start asking any investors to fund your venture.

Believe it or not, it's relatively easy to contact people who have the funds to invest in your show. We'll explain one way to do that in a moment. But it's a waste of time to even try contacting money providers until you're ready with convincing points about how you'll make their Benjamins eventually come back to them, and bring along some friends.

Your Show is a Real Business

If you want to secure an investor for your syndicated show, you need to think about your show like it is a real business. In reality, that's just what it is, when you boil it down. The product is your show. You need customers, and the first customers you need are listeners. You get them by signing up radio stations to carry your show.

Once listeners find you, the other set of customers you need are ad buyers. These are the customers who deliver the revenue. Their revenue will reward you and they'll reward the investor who backs the launch of your show.

This is basically the same formula as any other business. If you're opening a retail store, a restaurant, an art gallery, or whatever, you need good products. You need customers. You need to earn revenue. If your offer is solid, you'll get the customers. If you get enough customers, you'll earn lots of revenue.

How To Attract Capital

Launching any worthwhile business requires capital, an investment of dollars to get things going. But before the money is spent, you need a well thought out plan, including the steps to follow.

You need a review of the marketplace to explain how your business will serve a slice of that market. You need some intelligent estimates and projections of your costs and your expected results.

You need a timetable. This will show the expected startup, growth, and eventual success of your show. You may need a few qualified helpers to assist you in running things. All of these details go into your business plan. Lastly, you need to decide how you and the investor will be rewarded, once your show becomes popular.

For any investor (other than a family member or friend), the need to see a business plan is essential, before the checkbook is opened and the dollars are handed over to you.

So, how do you create a business plan for a syndicated radio show? You can get help from a competent accountant or business advisor. Or you can get a sample business plan specific to syndicated radio shows. We offer a sample 28 page business plan completely free of charge (along with more helpful info) at http://www.FreeRadioInfo.com.

Our free sample business plan is downloadable and is a DOC file so you can easily modify it for your show. Regardless of how you create a business plan, you will want to customize the details for your show and your particular situation. Having a template like ours to work from is a good way to get started.

How to Locate Investors

As you create your business plan, you'll learn more about the business of radio syndication than you ever did before. You'll have a clear picture of what must happen and when it must happen for you to succeed. Even better, your business plan will help convince an investor or financial institution to bankroll the project, get you started and on the road to success.

Now here is a way to locate investors to fund your venture. What's the secret? Very simply, visit your favorite search engine and type in the words "angel investor." Start checking the many options among the search results. There are people actively looking for places to invest their money.

You can also buy a book on how to find an angel investor for any startup venture. In a good economy or a bad economy, there is always money looking for promising investments. All you have to do is make the right connection.

One more approach: ask a local, financially successful person to back your venture. A local investor may seem more personal and friendly. Whether an investor is right next door or across the country, their money will be just as effective.

Getting the Bills Paid

Moving on now, let's quickly discuss a few more important ways to take care of business with a syndicated radio show. First, you can run all the ads in the world, but if you can't get the advertisers to pay for them, that's wasted time and effort. We're talking about receivables. These unpaid invoices can become a hassle if you don't stay on top of them. There are excellent books and websites with advice on getting customers to pay on a timely basis. Those are recommended reading.

Understand that in many cases, media buys such as radio show ads are not paid in advance. Most advertisers expect to be billed after the ads have run. But you can request payment in advance (or partial payment in advance), especially if the client is a small business or one you've never worked with before. If the advertiser refuses to pay in advance, you must decide if you want to extend payment terms.

In our experience, the vast majority of radio advertisers will pay you on time. However, if there's an ad agency involved in the process, the payments can take longer. In these cases, you may have a collection period of 30, 60, or 90 days. So, when it's June, you're being paid for the ads that ran in April. This is sometimes a fact of life with media sales, but on the plus side once money starts flowing it continues to flow.

Per the above example, in June you're paid for the spots from April. In July, you're paid for the spots in May, and so on. The cash flow tends to be constant once it begins, assuming the ads keep selling.

Again, the best way to deal with receivables is to stay on top of them. Frequent, friendly reminders are always the best way to get paid. In all the years we've been in this business, we can count on one hand the number of times that payments ran past 120 days. And we only got stiffed once, when a client suddenly went out of business. So don't worry needlessly about your receivables. Just watch them and at least every 30 days, send out written notices to those who haven't yet paid. Eventually in just about all cases, you will get the money.

Profits are waiting to be released from your show, as is the case of just about every well produced and targeted national radio show.

And let's mention another income-producing resource as we wrap up this chapter. We're talking about the **33X Sales Suite** video training that's free to you, as a reader of this book. To access the training, just visit http://www.FreeRadioInfo.com.

Chapter Sixteen

Promotion and Emotion

We have some tips and advice that might come in handy in planning the launch of a syndicated show.

First, seven words that may get a station executive to take a second look at your show: "Barter-free for the first six months." Everyone loves getting something for free. And if your show's just getting underway, you might not be able to sell those commercials yet anyway. So going barter-free for six months (or even 90 days) might be a good marketing angle for you to try.

Everybody Wants a Great Deal

If you think about your own purchasing decisions in today's economy, what are the ways that marketers get you to take action and purchase their product or service? One way that retailers long ago discovered to be extremely effective is to have a sale or offer a freebie deal of some kind to consumers.

For example, let's say a clothing store offers two pairs of pants or two dresses for the price of one. If you already like the store's products and you were thinking of buying anyway, that special deal might convince you to rush over to the store to spend your money.

You might ask, "Will a station put my show on the air just because there's no barter for the first six months?" Probably not, because that offer alone will not be a huge motivator. Different factors go into choosing a syndicated radio show. But if the station is already leaning in your direction, a deal like this might put your show over the top.

Web Site Suggestions

It's important that your show have a web site. Here's what should be included on your site. First, a page titled "About the Show." Tout all the great things about your show and what people say about it. Next, a page titled "About the Host" (or "Hosts"). A photo and short bio goes here.

You can include a page titled "Radio Stations" or "Radio Network". Here you might list all the stations that carry your show. Another option is to have visitors enter their zip code to find the nearest station.

You can even include a form so visitors can suggest a local station, if your show isn't already heard in their area. The visitor inputs the call letters of their favorite station, and you follow up by contacting the station. You tell the station that a listener suggested adding your show. We have seen stations positively respond to these suggestions.

Another page on your site might be titled "Stations Only." This could be where stations can hear your demo and download your marketing material. It could also be the page where affiliate stations download episodes of your show. You can set up this page with password protection if you wish, so the public can't access it.

Your site definitely should include a "Contact Us" page so visitors can get in touch with you.

Those are the barebones web site basics and you can certainly add more ideas to the site.

Five Money-Saving Steps

It's easy to spend money, but how about some ways to save some money while promoting your show? Here are five money-saving methods to promote your show.

Savings Step No. 1 - Write a Press Release

Pen a press release from time to time and email it to publications in your niche, as well as radio industry newsletters. It might get picked up for publication. But most everyone who gets it will look at it. This can generate good word of mouth attention for you. And if you're e-mailing your press releases, well, it costs you almost nothing. More about press releases in a moment.

Step No. 2 - Write an Article

You can write occasional articles focusing in your area of expertise and send them to publications for consideration. Let's just say you host a show on pets. You could write articles about pet care, trends in pet health, gifting pets to others, whatever. Pitch your articles to animal and pet related magazines and web sites. When they are picked up, this will enhance your credibility. You might even get paid for writing, or better yet get an offer for a regular column.

As a nationally syndicated host of a show on your niche topic, you are viewed as an authority on the topic. So why not take advantage of that perception? Of course, you can include copies of the articles in your station marketing after they are published, which makes you look like "the" expert.

Step No. 3 - Create an Email Newsletter

Think about creating an email newsletter that listeners can subscribe to on your web site. This allows you to remind them to listen to every episode of your show and helps you promote your upcoming guests and topics on your show.

Step No. 4 - Mass Mail a Postcard or One-sheet

As we mentioned previously, there are companies that specialize in mass mailing of postcards or other affordable promo pieces to a mailing list you provide. For very little per postcard, you can get your show seen by radio decision-makers. It's important to stay in front of your prospects and affordable mass mailings like this on a regular basis might make sense for you.

Step No. 5 - Generate Press Coverage

To wrap up our list of moneysaving ways to market your show, try using radio industry trade magazines and trade web sites to your advantage. Get to know the people who write the stories. Give them a call once in a while with a tip or idea for a column. They'll not only appreciate it, but you might find yourself getting unexpected mentions. That can only help your show grow. And when they need a pithy quote, they might just call you. Some industry sites allow reader comments to be posted, and you can use this to your advantage. Getting free press exposure takes nothing more than your time and a little effort.

Creating a Good Press Release

You might think that a press release is supposed to be all about you. Not so, if you want it to actually be used by journalists. The number one thing a release must contain is news, something that will capture a journalist's attention. You will get mentions because your release is the source of fresh news. Example, your show just signed a major station to carry your show. In the radio industry, that's news. Or you did a survey about your area of expertise and your release reveals the fascinating results. Or your release might tie in to a timely event such as the holiday season, Mother's Day, the release of a big new movie, or whatever. The timely tie in adds a current fresh element that improves the odds of your release being used as news.

Don't be afraid to jump out in front of a major story. Let's say there's a major national story making huge headlines. Come up with a genuinely clever new angle on that story and you just might hit the jackpot and grab some major big-time coverage. Journalists will probably identify you as a syndicated radio host and you might even end up on national TV, talking about your brilliant insight as the top news of the day. Some popular syndicated talk show hosts are particularly adept at working this angle and it sometimes gets them in the headlines.

Celebrities and National Buzz

Another way to grab attention is to somehow tie in with a nationally known person or organization that's related to the field of your show. Let's say you often interview top musicians on your show. You could do your show live from the Rock-and-Roll Hall of Fame. This would probably result in publicity and press coverage. Or let's say you host a political talk show, it's a presidential election year and you're able to get a candidate or two to appear on your show. An event like that would get your show covered by network and cable TV news. Or you could create a clever award or trophy of some type, and bestow it upon a leading citizen or politician to garner publicity for your show.

Put on your thinking cap and find ways to get national publicity. The fact is, the news these days is stranger than fiction. Many of today's headlines are begging for someone to take them one step further, or even parody them, if that's appropriate for your brand.

If you can find ways to tie in with today's headlines, you might grab a nice headline for yourself and that's sure to get your show noticed and possibly considered by radio stations.

Freebie Items

Swag – or as it's otherwise known, free stuff – is always appreciated by radio station people. Of course giving somebody a free cap, t-shirt, pen or calculator isn't going to get them to instantly add your show to their station, but it will get you noticed. If you can grab a few square inches of their valuable desktop real estate with a logo item, that radio decision-maker will see your logo all day every day, and this can only help your cause and keep you top of mind while others are forgotten or overlooked.

Attending Trade Shows

Another way to market your show is to attend radio trade shows and conventions. If you decide to do this, we can offer some ideas to make it worth your while. First, we do not suggest you buy a booth or floor space at an exhibition hall. While a booth may lend credibility, an unfortunate thing happens when you're tied to a booth. You're anchored in position. You lose mobility and the chance to capitalize on various opportunities as the crowd ebbs and flows at the show.

A booth does not let you plan for unforeseen problems. Let's say the booth next to yours has loud rock music or a bikini-clad team or free ice cream or some other distraction. This might put your booth at a disadvantage. You're also at the mercy of the flow of people. If for some reason few people come to the exhibition hall during a long afternoon because they're all someplace else, that time will be completely wasted for you.

Meet Everyone You Can

So what is the suggested way to attend trade shows? We suggest you (and perhaps your colleagues) go to the event with the goal of meeting as many people as possible. Bring along lots of business cards. You might also bring along a well thought out little gift that should be pocket-sized.

Meet as many radio decision-makers as you can. Give them your card (and the pocket sized gift if you have it). Tell them you'd like to follow up with them after the convention. Be sure to carry a pen and small notebook, as many of these executives will run out of their cards or won't have one to give to you. But you can jot down their name and call letters displayed on their badge, to follow up later.

Some syndicators who attend these trade shows bring along tons of sales materials. While radio executives might accept the materials and take it all back to their hotel rooms, they usually end up tossing it into the hotel room trash can rather than lug it home in their suitcase.

Follow Up After the Event

Once you return home, follow up quickly by sending your demo to the PDs you met at the trade show. Then follow up again by phone. This is a good combination of steps to follow. You began by meeting and talking with a decision-maker at the event. You then sent them a demo, and you followed up by phone. It puts you several steps ahead of the competition whose sales material is by now in a landfill near the convention city while your demo is sitting on the prospect's desk.

Other Giveaways

When it comes to marketing your show, what about other promotional gimmicks, gifts and giveaways? Well, let's consider one common item. Probably whatever your background, you have no doubt been the recipient of an imprinted coffee mug. These seem to be popular with just about everybody. Should you decide to follow the pack and give away a freebie travel mug or similar item, try to be original. Look for a unique design, better than average quality, and a multi-color imprint.

Consider imprinting the mug with a clever message relating to your show -- not just a boring logo. For example, let's say you do a show on finance and investing. You might imprint your mug with the bold words "Future Millionaire" on one side, and on the other your logo and web address. The bold message will make everyone smile and it will encourage your prospect to actually use the coffee mug. The same rules apply with any giveaway item you choose to send to prospects. Be original, be clever and go with the highest quality you can afford.

A popular promo item that gets used is the paper cube (or imprinted post-it note pack). Most people keep these on their desk and use them every day. With a paper cube, you could imprint your logo on all four sides, but don't do that. Use two sides for a clever, snappy message, and the other two sides for your logo and contact info. Everyone loves originality and creativity, especially radio people. Don't spend money to create a giveaway, and then be boring about it. Make it fun. And be sure to hire a good graphic artist to create a great look for your imprinted item.

Two Sets of Prospects

As a syndicator you have two sets of prospects – radio executives who may add your show to their stations and the radio listeners who may listen to your show. You have to appeal to both groups. There are endless ways to use promotional goodies to create buzz with both groups. You can stimulate listener response by offering items to callers. It will definitely get the phones ringing.

And as long as you're buying a load of items, order enough so you can send some to prospective station prospects, and to the stations that already carry your show. Gotta keep them happy, too.

Add That 'Emotional Hook'

In the Marketing Mindset chapter, we talked about how powerful an emotional hook can be in marketing any product or service. We mentioned companies like Disney and Revlon. These companies figured out the deep emotional need their services fulfill for customers and they use their marketing to point that out.

No doubt your show can find an emotional hook that will really connect with station executives and listeners. Your demo is where you can really tap into that power because it will be your primary marketing vehicle.

Let's say, for example, that you do a health show. Maybe the biggest emotional key to that topic is that this information helps save lives. Or let's say you do a show on animals. You can certainly hook into the emotional feelings people have toward their pets.

Figure out the hook that your show has. Ask listeners and really get to the heart of it and then use that angle in your demo materials. It will add the power of emotion to your marketing. Don't be afraid to tap into this emotional hook when you call stations. You may only have a few moments to get your point across. Don't be shy about hitting whatever the hot buttons are when a decision-maker is on the line and don't be afraid to show some emotion yourself. Go ahead and let your passion come through.

Why Stations Want Shows

Always remember that most program directors WANT syndicated radio shows. Why? Go back to what we said in Chapter One. Every fulltime radio station has 24 hours of programming time to fill, every single day. It's expensive and difficult to create 24 hours of good, quality programming on the typical radio station budget. Syndicated programming helps radio stations keep their listeners entertained and informed at a very low cost.

Secondly, most syndicated programs provide content that is impossible for a radio station to produce on their own. If you're an expert in your field, for example, what are the chances someone with your knowledge would be on the staff of a local radio station? So you can clearly see why syndication is in demand. This should encourage you to follow your dreams of syndication success.

Lastly, here are a few final words on the subject of turning your podcast into a broadcast. Your national audience and your ad income can only grow as fast as you do.

Since you're reading this book, you're obviously ready for growth. It's your choice to either do nothing when you finish reading this page, or to take action and follow through. A good first step is to visit http://www.FreeRadioInfo.com and claim the free files offered there.

If you want to contact us at Syndication Networks, we're here to help you. We offer a free strategy call to all qualified hosts. Just contact us at

http://SyndicationInfo.com

Turn to the last pages of the book for more details on our services. We hope to hear from you soon.

APPENDIX

Sample Program Clock and Notes

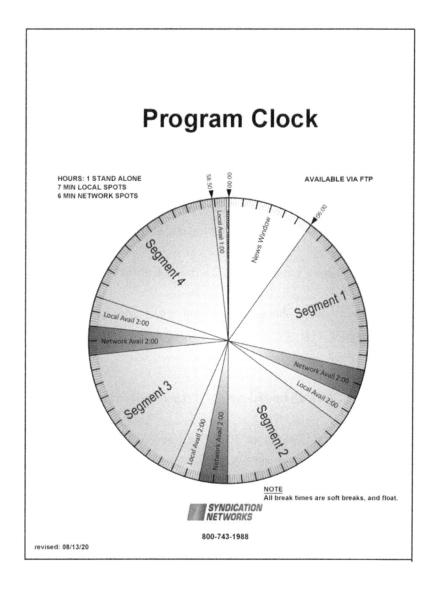

Program Clock

HOURS: 1 STAND ALONE
7 MIN LOCAL SPOTS
6 MIN NETWORK SPOTS

AVAILABLE VIA FTP

58:50   00:00

06:00

Local Avail 1:00

News Window

Segment 4

Segment 1

Local Avail 2:00

Network Avail 2:00

Network Avail 2:00

Local Avail 2:00

Segment 3

Local Avail 2:00

Network Avail 2:00

Segment 2

NOTE
All break times are soft breaks, and float.

SYNDICATION
NETWORKS

800-743-1988

revised: 08/13/20

159

Every Clock Page Needs Five Essentials

If you have a long form show, create a clock page that shows the various elements in your show and when they happen. It's common for program directors to ask for a show clock. The most common style is simply a big circle or pie chart, showing when the various segments happen, similar to slices of pie. For any long form show, the clock page is the source of key information.

The typical clock includes the following five pieces of information.

Show Clock Essential No. 1 - Number of Ad Minutes

First, the number of local and national ad minutes within the hour. This is important for station programming, sales and traffic departments.

Show Clock Essential No. 2 – Your Contact Information

The show contact phone number and email address are needed in case of emergency. If something goes wrong, stations like to know they can contact somebody.

Show Clock Essential No. 3 - Tech Details of Distribution

The satellite, download or FTP distribution information. This is important since the person who sets up your show on their local station can't be expected to remember exactly how to get your show. (They may air a dozen or more other syndicated shows, all with different clocks and different sources.)

Show Clock Essential No. 4 - Cues, Cutaways, Promos, IDs

Fourth, the key details on cues into and out of breaks, cutaways, promo positions, and station I.D.s. These tell the local station when to insert their commercials and legal station id's, etc. without stepping on your show and your national commercials.

Show Clock Essential No. 5 - Names of Syndicator and Show

Fifth, identify the producer and/or syndicator, not only so the station can contact you but also to brand your identity with the station.

It's amazing how much information is packed onto some clock pages by syndicators. Just try to design your clock so it's readable and understandable. You might have a talented graphics person design your clock page so it's easy to quickly scan and pleasing to the eye.

As a reader of this book, you get an instant free download of Power Tools, including these documents to syndicate your show:

- Sample Station Agreement
- Station Marketing Kit
- Advertiser Media Kit
- Advertising Agreement
- Sample Rate Card

- Station Welcome Letter
- Sample Program Release
- Station Pitch Letters
- Download memos
- And Much More!

Free Syndication Business Plan

Business Plan prep is much easier with our sample 28 page Radio Syndication BUSINESS PLAN. Download it for free, update the plan with your info, and use it to fund your syndication project.

Plus a free video training that has dozens of money-making ideas for your radio show or podcast.

Download these Power Tools now at
www.FreeRadioInfo.com

TURN YOUR PODCAST INTO A BROADCAST

The people at Syndication Networks are experts at turning podcasts into nationally syndicated radio shows. We've been in business for over 25 years.

Our turn key service includes signing up stations, ad sales, and national marketing as a package.

Our team will sign up stations to carry your show. Once your show has a national audience, we can sell ads in your show, earning you profits.

You simply do your show, and we do the rest.

Visit Us to Learn More:

http://SyndicationInfo.com

Made in the USA
Las Vegas, NV
21 January 2021

16311908R00095